The
Art of Sculling

FEB   1992

stat

The
Art of Sculling

by

Joe Paduda

Photographs by

Les Henig

International Marine Publishing
Camden, Maine

Published by International Marine Publishing

10 9 8 7 6 5 4 3 2 1

Copyright © 1992 International Marine Publishing, an imprint of TAB BOOKS. TAB Books is a division of McGraw-Hill, Inc.

Library of Congress Cataloging-in-Publication Data
    Paduda, Joe.
        The art of sculling/Joe Paduda; photographs
    by Les Henig.
            p.   cm.
        Includes index.
        ISBN 0-87742-308-3
        1. Rowing.   I. Title.
    GV791.P28   1992
    797.1'23—dc20   91-30853
                                            CIP

Questions regarding the content of this book should be addressed to:

International Marine Publishing
P.O. Box 220
Camden, ME 04843

Text design by Patrice M. Rossi
Printed and bound by Donnelley, Harrisonburg, VA

Contents

To my father,
the finest man
I ever knew

Acknowledgments

I have gotten immense satisfaction from sculling, and I wrote this book to help others do the same. A lot of people helped write this book, many of whom didn't know they were doing so at the time. They gave freely of their time and expertise not for any material gain but because they felt it was important to contribute something to the sport that had given so much to them. I wrote this book to try to repay the sport by passing that knowledge along to the next group of aspiring novices.

I would like to single out a few people whose assistance greatly improved the quality of *The Art of Sculling*. If and when you find something within these pages that seems insightful and crystal clear, your appreciation should be directed to the folks identified below. Where things are more obtuse, your author is to be credited.

Jim Wells is a great friend and a terrific editor. To say that Jim's insights into every aspect of sculling were invaluable is to do him a disservice. I am truly grateful for his help.

Jay Printzlau is the best coach I've ever known. He taught his oarsmen that the only limitations are self-imposed and gave us the confidence to push the limits every piece.

The people who taught me to scull, the athletes I raced, the coaches who cajoled, begged, and threatened, the teammates I had the honor of training and competing with all had a part in this, and I thank all of you.

Thanks also to the athletes who consented to share their expertise by posing for pictures. They are: Dave Paduda, Jim Wells, Phil Yeich, Brad Halterman, Jim Ferrell, John Gilbert, John Schintzel, and Elizabeth Webber.

Les Henig, who shot most of the photos for this book, was a pleasure to work with.

Jon Eaton at International Marine Publishing actually thought a book on sculling might sell. I appreciate his willingness to take a chance on an author whose published works consisted of a letter to the editor of *The Washington Post*. Jon's gambler's instinct, patience, and gentle suggestions have been much appreciated.

Elise Earl and Tom McCarthy are the people who translated my verbiage into cohesive, coherent text, and did so with the utmost tact.

My mom was and is a great supporter, both emotionally and substantively. Not only did she help with the editing, she also compiled the index when I couldn't bear the thought of looking at the manuscript ever again.

Finally, my wife, Debbie, was a true teammate. Her understanding when I left the dishes on the table, our daughter in her arms, and disappeared into the den for hours on end made this possible.

Introduction

Sculling is the rarest of vocations. Without fail it provides a reward precisely indexed to the amount of effort invested. And the process is constant: Each stroke is a measure of the sculler's skill, dedication, and concentration. Your successes in a single shell are your own; your successes in a team boat are a measure of your adaptability, skill, and patience.

The instant and constant feedback that sculling provides is a refreshing contrast to almost everything else we do. No one else's opinion matters, neither do petty politics, what you did yesterday or last week, the school you went to and the grades you got, where you live, or what car you drive. You alone control how well you scull, and your ability is continuously tested.

Sculling offers respite from the increasingly complex challenges of basic everyday life. Sculling is such an intense sensory and analytical experience that one has no time to dwell on other matters. You feel the wheels of the slide turning under you, pressure on the tops of your feet as you pull yourself up to the catch, your weight hanging on the oars as the blades bite the water the instant the drive begins. You hear your labored breathing, the water murmuring under the boat, and the soft sounds of the catch and release that announce your efficiency. You sense the wind pressing on your blades as you roll them up to the catch, and see the water ripple. Your arms and legs begin to tire as the end of the workout approaches and the lactic acid builds—and burns—in your quads. You watch the clock, steer around the rocks just upstream, track the progress of your competitors, monitor the stroke rate and work on getting your hands out of bow just a little bit faster.

With all this going on it can be very difficult to concentrate. There is too much to assimilate, to analyze, to act on instantaneously. It is too easy to be overwhelmed by the sensory flood. If you are to improve beyond a basic level of competence, you will have to learn to discern between the important and the trivial, and to focus on what you are doing at that instant. You must realize that there are no distinct components of the stroke: The catch, the drive, the release, and the recovery are inseparable. Even when you focus on one aspect of the stroke you'll sense its effect on the rest of the stroke. You will learn that one movement, correctly executed, leads to other movements correctly executed.

The purpose of this book is to provide you with the knowledge of the science of sculling, help you comprehend the mechanics of a technically correct stroke, and give you a solid understanding of the physiology of the sport. It's up to you to take the information, apply it, and make yourself the best sculler you have the time and inclination to become.

That process is the art of sculling.

Chapter One

First Row

Sculling can be a true pleasure, especially if you have some idea what you are doing. This chapter will help you get started the right way with a fun first row. And it is supposed to be fun. Don't worry about memorizing all the details now; they'll come back to you at the appropriate time. The important thing to remember when you are just starting is that everyone looked as bad as you do and felt as awkward, and swore repeatedly they would never get it right. When I first started sculling I promised myself many times I would never go out again if I could just make it back to the dock in a vertical position. This after eight years of rowing in eights, fours, and pairs. So, if you are just getting started in rowing, take it a stroke at a time. It will get better. You'll surprise yourself one day by realizing you aren't doing so badly after all.

You are preparing for your first row. You have made the correct sacrifices to the river or lake gods, are wearing appropriate attire, and have determined that the weather is not threatening. First, take your sculls (oars) down to the dock and put them on the dock where you won't step on them. Carry the oars with the blades in front of you, where you can see them and avoid bumping them into something or someone. If you have to extricate them from a tight spot, be careful and watch both ends of the oars.

Always carry the oars with the blades in front of you.

You are now back in the boathouse or standing next to your car, looking at the boat as if for the first time. The first thought that crosses your mind is, "How do I carry this thing?" It is long, unwieldy, may belong to someone else, and has plastic or metal arms sticking out from the sides. If you have conned a friend into accompanying you on this auspicious occasion, the solution is simple. He'll grab one end, you the other, and off you go. Since many sculling boats weigh more than you can handle alone, this may be a good idea. You'll be a lot happier if you arrange for some assistance than if you drop the boat.

If you have decided to avoid the peals of laughter certain to be directed at you during this first row and are thus alone, don't despair. Take your time and use good judgment.

Many sculling boats are relatively light, so you may feel confident you can handle it alone. If the boat is on the ground or a low rack, set up slings next to it, making sure you check both ends before moving it. Since it's probably upside down, put one hand on each side of the boat, grasping the gunwales. Test your hand position for balance by lifting slightly. Pick up the boat, step back, and put it in the slings. Roll the boat over so it is hull down (also called guts up). Locate the handles built into the boat and grab hold. If there don't seem to be any handles, select two sturdy crossbraces or other structural supports. Again, test your balance by lifting slightly. Once you are satisfied that you have a well-balanced grip, lift up the boat, balancing it on your head. Hint: Don't wear one of those baseball hats with a little metal button at the top. It will be pressed into your skull, with obvious unpleasant results.

With one hand on a rigger (the plastic or metal arm sticking out from the gunwale) and the other steadying the boat, carry the boat down to the dock. Watch the riggers and the doorways, trees, and other scullers. Also, don't make any sharp turns without making sure the bow and stern are clear of obstacles.

Some folks prefer to carry the boat at their side while their hands remain on the selected grips. Others like to carry the boat balanced on a shoulder. Any way is fine. Remember to go slow and pay attention.

If the boat is in a rack, make sure you check both ends before moving it.

Make sure you spread the slings far enough apart so the washbox is clear.

You are standing on the dock, facing the water with your toes over the edge and with a boat on your head or shoulder. Check the dock and water for obstacles and make sure you are clear of other shells. Grab the handles again, lift the boat off your head or shoulder and drop it to your waist. Place the boat gently in the water, making sure the fin on the bottom of the hull (if there is one) is clear of the dock. You may want to place the bow or stern in the water first and slide the boat in.

Most launching areas require boats to launch in one direction, so make sure you know which direction is correct. The steps necessary to launch and land from the starboard, or right side, of the boat follow.

Before you get in the boat, make sure all the porthole covers and other watertight seals are tightly closed. Some boats have four of these: one in the bow of the cockpit in front of the tracks, another under the tracks in the footwell, yet another aft of (to the stern of) the footstretchers, and a plug in the very tip of the stern.

Once all is secure, place the oars in the oarlocks, making sure the keepers (the things that hold the oars in) are closed. Push the oars all the way out into the oarlocks and grasp both handles with your right hand. Make sure the port oar blade is flat on the water, since the boat is much more stable that way.

Look in the cockpit to determine the appropriate place to step into the boat. In many boats, there are clearly marked places you should not step. If there are no such markings, you should be able to step between the tracks without fear. Do not step anywhere else; never step directly in the bottom of the boat.

Step into the boat with your right foot while holding onto the dock with your left hand. Now, as gracefully as possible, transfer all your weight onto your right leg and settle into the seat while putting your left foot into the shoe.

If you are uncomfortable with this maneuver, feel free to sit on the edge of the dock and slide your rear end onto the seat. Less graceful, but you can save your grace for your sculling.

Congratulations! You are now sitting in a rowing shell, perhaps for the first time. It probably seems quite a bit less stable than you would like. It is. Put your fears

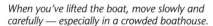

When you've lifted the boat, move slowly and carefully — especially in a crowded boathouse.

You can also use the riggers as handles.

behind you, adjust your footstretchers to fit, and you are ready to go.

Actually, the easiest way to adjust the stretchers is while the boat is still in slings, but since this is your first row, you don't know what the ideal adjustment is. Set the stretchers so that you almost hit the front stops on the tracks when you are drawn all the way up on the slide. Then, to make sure you are going to be in the right position at the finish of the stroke, straighten your legs and lean back slightly while grasping the oar handles. Once you're comfortable, secure your feet. Again, don't let go of the oars at any time. Place the handles between your knees and chest while fiddling with the stretchers and rest the outboard blade flat on the water.

Almost ready. Check the keepers once more to make sure they are tight, get comfortable on the seat, maintain your grasp on the oars with your right hand, and shove off from the dock with your left hand. Give the dock a good shove; if you

Keep your weight over the dock when you lock the far oarlock.

Don't ever let go of the oars when getting into — or out of — a boat.

With your hands drawn to your chest, your thumbs should just brush your shirt.

It's safer to get tied in before you launch — the boat's a lot more stable at the dock.

don't, you will be stuck halfway out on the water floundering around until the wind blows you off the dock or someone comes along to help. If you don't clear the dock on the first shove, carefully push yourself away from the dock with the starboard oar.

Clear of the dock, paranoia may set in. The boat seems a lot smaller than when it was on your head, and quite tippy. The key is to relax and keep both blades flat on the water. Even though sitting in a boat for the first time is an awkward, unsteady, unnatural feeling, relax your arms, back, and hands and just sit there for a moment. When your heart rate has dropped to a normal pace, try raising one hand slightly and lowering the other while still holding onto the oars. You will notice the boat leaning toward the side on which you have dropped your hand.

More congratulations are in order: This is your first lesson on controlling the boat, and one that will serve you well. You have just learned that the proper way to control the balance of the boat is not by leaning to one side, but by raising or lowering the hands and thus, the oars. When the boat is down to one side, simply raise that hand slightly, lower the other, and the boat will right itself.

It's now time for your first stroke. Your legs should be straight, not bent, and you should be sitting in a relaxed position with your back straight but not rigid. Your hands are at the ends of the oar handles, the thumb over the end of the handle and the handle resting in the fingers (no white knuckles). When the blade is square (perpendicular to the water), the wrists should be flat, not bent up or down. This position makes for the most comfortable, as well as the strongest, grip. Don't worry about feathering the oars yet; we'll get to that later.

By now you have noticed that your hands overlap. While this may seem awkward, it is necessary due to the mechanics of the boat. Simply cross your left hand over your right.

With your arms extended, raise both hands until the blades are just covered with water, pull your hands into your body, push them down, and extend your arms. Repeat, making sure you are moving both hands simultaneously. Do this ten times or so, then stop with both blades flat on the water. Relax and start over again. Pretty soon you will find you can do this without too much trouble.

Be careful to push straight out, especially when the wind is pushing you back into the dock.

You'll notice the boat tipping with even a slight change in hand position.

Cradle the oar handle in your fingers, don't clench it in your palms. Even at full pressure the grip should be relaxed.

Notice that the wrists are flat as the oars are pulled through the water and that the back leans just a few degrees toward the bow.

Up to this point you have been rowing "arms only." Now, add the back. From the finish (hands drawn in to your body, back leaning slightly toward the bow, legs straight) square the blades, and extend your arms. Pivot forward from your hips and put the oars in the water. Keeping your arms extended, lean back until you are in the finish position. Pull the oars in with your arms and push your hands down. Repeat this motion ten times, stop, and try it again. Keep this up until you feel reasonably comfortable.

The arms and back contribute two-thirds of the stroke sequence. To complete the stroke, add your legs. From the finish position, extend your arms and bend forward from the hips, then draw yourself forward with your legs. At the catch, your shins will be vertical, your chest on your knees, and your arms fully extended with the blades squared up, ready to enter the water.

To recap from the finish, or release of the water: Arms out, back up, legs up, catch, then reverse the sequence for the drive. A good way of implanting this in your memory is by rote. From the catch position (leaning forward with your legs drawn up), repeat "legs, back, arms." Drop your hands to remove the oars from the water,

The back is always straight, but not stiff; the motion is a pivot from the hips, not a rounding of the back.

The blade should leave the water squared up.

Prepared for the catch: The final motion will be an unweighting of the hands as the blades drop in the water.

Make sure the opposite blade is flat on the water during the turn.

You can stop more quickly by forcefully pushing your blades (slightly squared) into the water.

and repeat "arms, back, legs." Of course, the transition points are not as sharply defined as described here, but keep them that way for now to implant them in your muscular memory.

Turning and stopping are two skills you'll need to learn. For now, the easiest and simplest turn is to continue sculling but pull harder on one side than the other.

You can also stop and scull the boat around with your arm and back, pulling one oar while the other rests with its blade flat on the water.

If you need to stop in a hurry, bury both blades in the water and lock your arms in whatever position they happen to be in. The most stable position is with your legs flat, your back straight or leaning slightly toward the bow, and your arms holding the oar handles close to your body.

Make sure you pause every few strokes to look around. You aren't the only one out there, so be aware of where you are and of your direction at all times.

Don't try to do too much on your first row. Stay out for a half-hour or so. If your arms and shoulders tire, relax your grip on the oars and lower your shoulders. You will see many novice scullers in the turtle position, their shoulders touching their ears. If you find yourself doing likewise, stop and relax before continuing.

When it's time to navigate your way back to the dock, don't be concerned with how it looks. Ideally you want to row toward the dock at a slight angle, stop rowing a few feet out and glide in. Make sure the oar opposite the dock is flat on the water, keep the blade on the dockside high enough to clear, and reach out and grab the dock with your left hand. Considering this is your first trip out, don't be concerned if your landing is somewhat less than ideal.

Once at the dock, remove your feet from the stretchers, hold on to both oars with the right hand, put your right foot under you, rise up on your right foot and out of the boat with your left. With your right foot still in the boat and your left arm holding the starboard rigger to the dock, reach out and unlock the port oarlock. Take the oars out and set them in a safe place where you won't step on them. Finally, with both feet on the dock, take hold of the handles or gunwales, lower your rear end, and, using your legs, lift the boat out of the water. Place the boat on slings or, if need be, on the dock until help arrives. Don't try to lift the boat by bending over from the waist and using your back muscles.

Wash off the boat, wipe it down, and put it away. Get your sculls from the dock, wipe them down, and put them in the rack. Good job!

By dragging the outside (port) oar you can swing the stern in toward the dock.

Don't let go of the oars until you are safely on the dock.

You can unlock the keeper from the dock provided you keep your weight on the dock.

Don't try to lift the boat by bending over and using your back — lift with your legs.

Chapter Two

Beginning Technique

ow that you are familiar, if not comfortable, with your boat and the whole idea of sculling, it's time to learn more about sculling. You may want to develop your skills to the point where you can race competitively, or perhaps you just want to develop enough proficiency to enjoy a weekly exercise row on the water or on the hi-tech rowing machines at the local health club.

Whoever you are and whatever category you place yourself in, if you can do most of the things discussed in this chapter reasonably well, you will be able to get more from your sculling.

One of the sport's most important lessons reveals that it's a lot easier to go fast by sculling well than by pulling hard. The problem is it is easier to pull hard than it is to row well, and you will go faster sooner if you ignore technique and just pull hard. Unfortunately, sculling well takes time to learn. Take the time to learn how to scull correctly and you will never forget. Insist on being macho, and you will find that while you may go faster sooner, you will reach a plateau quickly and never get much better. When you finally decide to learn how to scull correctly, you will end up investing much more time and energy correcting ingrained problems.

CONCENTRATION AND RELAXATION

The secret to good technique can be found in two words: concentration and relaxation. Scullers with good powers of concentration get more out of each workout. The reason is simple: by concentrating on each stroke and each movement within the stroke you implant the correct movement in your "neuro-muscular memory." If, on the other hand, your mind wanders and you worry about work, checkbook balances, or the pennant race, you are wasting your time. In fact, you are probably better off not sculling at all. The reason for this lies in the body's method of learning and "memorizing" a sequence of movements.

Just as your body learns the movements that are correct technique by repeating the motions over and over, it will adopt poor technique if you are not focused on what you are doing. The longer you scull with flaws in your technique, the harder it becomes to correct them.

Consistency comes to those with good concentration. Consistency is as general as sculling on a regular schedule and as specific as pulling through each stroke at the same height. You are much better off sculling fairly well but consistently than if you only row well occasionally. With consistency you can correct whatever technical flaws you may have and be secure in the knowledge that once you have the correct motion implanted in your muscular memory, you'll not have to consciously force yourself to scull correctly.

The second key to good sculling is relaxation. A rigid, tense sculler is wasting mental and physical energy and slowing the boat by not allowing it to glide smoothly on the recovery. The rigid sculler is probably not having a good time, either. Conversely, a relaxed sculler is not anxious, does not waste energy, allows the boat to work for him, and is able to anticipate changing conditions and adapt to them quickly and easily. There are many different ways to relax. Although you'll have to find the way that works best for you, a simple, pre-set plan will eliminate a lot of stress on the water.

Before launching, sit down and review what you want to accomplish. It may be anything from winning the Masters Nationals to sculling five strokes without crabbing. Whatever it is, you can now begin the workout with a set goal in mind and a set plan for attaining that goal. By setting your workouts in advance you will be able to focus your energies on what you want to accomplish and not waste time on the water.

Once on the water, you may find yourself, for whatever reason, getting tense. If possible, stop sculling, sit easy in the boat, take three very long, slow, deep breaths, remind yourself of your goals and plan for the workout, and begin sculling again. If it's not possible to stop, consciously tell yourself to relax. One effective way to remind yourself to relax is to repeat a word or phrase, either out loud or in your mind, that you associate with relaxation.

Finally, stay "in the boat" at all times. Stay focused on what you are out there to accomplish, on how the boat feels, on water and wind conditions, and on your surroundings. Don't waste water time concerning yourself with the complexities of your off-the-water existence; it will still be there when you get back to the dock. Use water time to improve your sculling and let the rest of your life wait for the end of the row.

There are two components of technique: bladework and bodywork. While the two are inextricably linked, they are separated here for the sake of simplifying the sculling motion. At the end of each of the following sections is a list of drills designed to help you with different aspects of technique. If your sculling doesn't seem to be going well, you may find it helpful to refer back to these drills in the future

BODYWORK

You'll recall from your inaugural row that the sequence for body motion (from the catch) is drive the legs, then the back, then the arms. The recovery is the opposite: arms out, then back, and finish the recovery by drawing the legs up. The motion is not separated and disjointed; all your movement in a boat should be fluid and smooth with all but imperceptible transition points. Ideally, everything finishes together. The timing is sequential, but with shading. When the legs are approximately halfway down, on the drive portion of the stroke, the back begins to open up, or lean back toward the bow. Just after the back begins to open up, the arms break, pulling the handles in to the body.

This "connected" body motion accomplishes several things. First, it employs the body's muscle groups in a descending order of strength. During the stroke cycle, the boat speeds up and slows down as the sculler pulls the oars through the water, releases the water, and moves back up the slide on the recovery. At the catch the boat is at the slowest point in the cycle, so the largest and strongest muscle group (the legs) is used to get the boat moving again. As the boat begins to pick up speed from the sculler's leg drive, the back begins to open up, adding to the shell's momentum. Finally, the arms, the weakest muscles, finish the drive, pulling the oars in to the body quickly and smoothly.

The drive is over, and the sculler now begins the recovery process. This part of the cycle is aptly named, as the recovery performs two functions. First, the sculler moves himself back into position to begin the next drive. Second, this is his only chance to rest while the boat moves forward on its own, or "runs out." Ideally, the sculler can relax for an instant and prepare himself for the next stroke while garnering the most run possible from his boat.

The recovery is the most important part of the stroke. It receives less attention than it should from almost everyone, perhaps because it is the only time the boat

The legs are almost down, the back is near the finish position, and the arms are completing the pull-through.

The legs have started the drive at the instant the blades enter the water.

At the point the legs are almost finished, the back is halfway through its motion, and the arms have begun to pull in.

works for you, instead of the other way around. Pay a lot of attention to the recovery; to belabor a point made above, it is a lot easier to row well than it is to pull hard, and you'll go faster too.

At the release, get your hands away from the body quickly and smoothly. The boat is moving fastest at this point, and quick hands will help to maintain that speed. You will also notice that the boat is sitting low in the water at the release. This is because you have just transferred all of your weight into the bow, driving it down into the water. So, get those hands out of bow!

The arms should be pushed away from the body until they are almost straight. Keep them bent slightly; this will allow you to absorb any shocks from your oars striking rough water without unduly disturbing the boat's balance. When the arms are extended, pivot forward from the hips until the hands pass over the knees. At this point, the legs start bending as you draw yourself up toward the catch. At the catch, your shins should be vertical, your chest touching your knees, and your arms straight. This position is the most precarious in the stroke cycle. It is very difficult to correct balance problems once you are at the catch, so be sure you have the boat set up before you get there.

The hands lead the body out of bow, the back is straight, and the legs are still flat.

Level hands help set the boat on an even level on the recovery.

The catch position is perfect, but notice the waves coming from the hull. A rushed slide has bounced the boat down into the water, slowing it.

On the recovery, do not fling yourself into the stern with abandon. Instead, pull yourself up the slide with your toes. Compared to the hand motion on the recovery, the legs move slowly, with control. A controlled slide will give you the last little bit of run in the boat. A rushed slide will slow you down tremendously, as you are transferring all of your weight very quickly to the stern. The net effect of this transfer is to drive the hull down into the water, increasing the boat's friction as it moves through the water and slowing it down.

The entire stroke sequence should be marked by no pause or hesitation, no matter how slight. The cycle is a continuous movement, with no part of the cycle rushed or jerky. Envision the body's motion during the stroke as something not unlike crouching down, picking something up, and then standing.. You can't discern a clear end of the movement down or the beginning of the movement up.

Don't expect your stroke to be smooth, controlled, coordinated and powerful immediately. What you are looking for is gradual improvement each time you row. As with anything else, you will reach plateaus where you don't seem to get any better. When you get stuck on one of these, go back to the basics. By thinking about each part of your stroke and comparing it to the ideal, you will probably identify the problem. Then use the drills described below to make corrections, and resume your quest for perfection.

Drills for Bodywork

Pause Drill.

Purpose: To slow down the stroke cycle to enable the sculler to focus on each stroke; the sculler can then make technical corrections and modifications and see the results in the next stroke. Useful for identifying technical flaws.

Description: This drill can utilize a pause in the stroke at any position, from hands in at the finish to fully extended at the catch. Typical pause points are with the hands away, with the back leaning toward the stern, and at half slide. A pause at the finish is not recommended as it may encourage the sculler to keep the hands in bow instead of moving them away from the body immediately.

A pause with the hands away is useful for ensuring that the hands come away quickly and smoothly from the finish, reaching almost full extension before the legs start to bend. Similarly, a pause with the back leaning over toward the stern can help make sure the maximum body angle is achieved early on in the stroke cycle. The half-slide pause is designed to allow the sculler to pause and check body angle, handle height, and overall balance just before the catch.

Process: Sculling at one-quarter pressure or greater, pause briefly every stroke at the specific point selected. During the pause, review the preceding stroke and decide what modifications will be made in the next stroke. Focus on one detail at a time; you can't fix all your technical flaws at one time.

After you have mastered the correction and are incorporating it in your stroke consistently, try two strokes at a time. Move to three, and then row continuously to see if the correction has "stuck."

Fast Hands.

Purpose: To emphasize the hand speed out of bow.

Description: Scull at any pressure with the hands moving away from the body very quickly. Try to move them twice as fast as usual.

Process: Incorporate this drill into practice routines, rowing with fast hands at least five minutes per workout.

Bladework

Ah, the nemesis of the hammer and the winning ticket for the old, weak, and out of shape. Many oarsmen somewhat lacking in technical proficiency have been successful in spite of their poor technique. Do not make the mistake of believing that you, too, can succeed without paying attention to the finer points of style. You may be able to go fast, win races, or have fun rowing on flat water, over short distances, or against mediocre opponents, but you will quickly achieve your not-very-fast maximum speed. While everyone else improves, you will be stuck at your plateau. Not until you learn to scull well will you get any faster.

Simply put, bladework involves putting the oar in the water with the blade squared up at the catch, removing it from the water still squared up, feathering it as soon as the blade has cleared the water, and gradually rolling the blade up so it is ready for the next stroke. Piece of cake.

You are sitting easily in the boat in the finish position. The blades are resting flat on the water, arms are drawn in to the body, back in bow, legs flat. The oar handles are resting lightly in the first joint of your fingers, thumbs over the ends of the handles. This is the position they should be in for the entire recovery. Do not make the common mistake of gripping the oars tightly in a clench reminiscent of rigor mortis; if you do, you'll find yourself afflicted with Popeye-like forearms.

Lower your hands so the blades are off the water and the boat is balanced by the weight of the oars.

The blade is almost square as the hands pass over the shoes.

At the catch, the hands should be positioned on the sculls so the wrists are flat and the handles are resting in the fingers.

The hands will almost graze each other as the arms pull through.

Lower your hands so the blades are off the water and the boat is balanced by the weight of the oars. Begin the recovery by extending the arms and pivoting the back toward the stern. Bend the legs and start slowly up the slide. When your hands cross over your ankles, begin to roll the oar handles up into your hands. The blades should be completely rolled up before you are at the catch, so all you have to do is raise the hands slightly to have a perfect catch.

At the catch, the hands should be positioned on the sculls so the wrists are flat and the handles are resting in the fingers. As you begin the drive, the hands act as connectors, transmitting the power of the legs, back, and arms directly to the sculls.

Just after the arms begin to break, the left hand crosses over the right. For some reason novice scullers are apprehensive about this part of the stroke, but this apprehension quickly passes. Sometimes, especially in rough water, the hands will crash into each other. As with any other mishap, just relax, continue sculling, and be glad your trimmed your fingernails that morning. If you didn't, you may find yourself with several nasty scratches across the back of your right hand.

You have almost completed the drive and are now rapidly approaching the finish, or release. At the instant the legs go down, the back finishes swinging into bow and the arms finish drawing the oar handles in to the body; the hands push down and then, and only then, away from the body. If you try to push the hands away and down simultaneously, you will undoubtedly "throw a lip" of white water when the oars get caught in the water. Remember, the oars are moving in the opposite direction, and quickly. If you don't get them out of the water quickly, they will get caught between you (the immovable object) and the water moving past you (the irresistible force). Sometimes you'll win. When the water wins, you will "catch a crab" and drastically slow the boat down as you struggle to get the blades out of the water and away from your body. Avoid this unnecessary flailing around by dropping your hands quickly and smoothly at the finish. As soon as the blades clear the water, feather the oars—that is, roll them so the blades are parallel to the water.

Turning and stopping are two additional skills you'll have to learn. The easiest and simplest turn you've already used: Continue sculling but pull harder on one side than the other. You can also stop and scull the boat around with your arm and back pulling one oar while the other rests, blade feathered, on top of the water. To speed up the turn, square the resting blade and drag it in the water. Not too deep or you'll be swimming. Again, use the arm and back only to scull the boat around.

The fastest way to turn the boat, and the one using the smallest turning radius, alternates between backing with one oar and sculling with the other. You can use a half slide for this if you so desire.

By now, you have probably figured out how to stop a boat. You can stop a boat very quickly by burying both squared blades in the water. Don't make a habit of this since it may unduly stress your boat, which is designed to handle the stress of hard pulling, not stopping.

Drills for Bladework

The drills discussed in the section on bodywork can also be useful for developing or refining your bladework. When you tire of focusing on the body motions in a specific drill, concentrate on the bladework for an additional 20 strokes. This will help you get the maximum benefit from the drill.

Blades Square.

Purpose: To force the sculler to move the hands down and then away from the body at the finish of the stroke and to keep the hands low throughout the recovery. This is especially important if you always scull on flat water.

Description: Scull without feathering the oars at any time. Make sure not to cheat by slightly feathering the blade to make the finish easier, as this flaw is exactly what the drill is designed to correct. Be sure to pull the oars in high, then quickly and smoothly push the hands down and away from the body. Lyons Bradley, sculling coach at Undine Barge Club, likens the finish motion to that of a bicycle chain moving quickly and smoothly down and then away from the rear sprocket.

Process: Incorporate several minutes of blade square rowing in each workout. Try to do some blades square sculling during the pressure part of the practice so it will carry over to racing or rowing hard.

Good blade-square sculling. The hands are level so the boat is level.

Hands on the Loom.

Purpose: To exaggerate the feathering movement of the hands to help the sculler learn the correct motions.

Description: Slide the hands down onto the wooden or fiberglass part of the oar, several inches below the handle. Continue sculling at light pressure, feel the hands as they roll the sculls up to the catch, lift at the catch, and push down and away at the finish.

Process: Try this only when the water is flat and warm enough to swim in. A few minutes of sculling with the hands in this position is all that is really necessary to be beneficial.

Feet-out Sculling.

Purpose: To ensure that the release is as clean and smooth as possible.

Description: Rest the feet on top of the shoes. Scull continuously at a light pressure and a low rating. Be careful at the release since you haven't tied into the boat. Also, be aware that a normal recovery will not be possible since you can't pull yourself up the slide with your toes. I've sculled several miles this way and found that it cleaned up the release tremendously.

Process: Try this only when the water is flat and warm enough to swim in. Scull with your feet out for several minutes at a time. Make this a standard part of your workout early in the season, and use the drill once or twice a week after that, especially if your release is getting sloppy.

Hands-on-the-loom drill: The hands should be a couple of inches below the grips. Don't reach too far.

Feet-out drill: The key to remaining dry is to keep pressure on the oar handles all the way through the stroke.

Chapter Three

Equipment

nfortunately, sculling equipment can be quite expensive and hard to locate. Fortunately, once you have acquired a boat and oars, your expenditures are minimal—unless you make a habit of running into large and unyielding objects.

Of course, one can buy an incredible amount of paraphernalia that some might deem essential, such as heart-rate meters, clothing, compasses, rear-view mirrors, car racks, boat covers, and the like. That is up to the individual; what you really need is access to a decent boat and a set of sculls matched to that boat.

Sculling boats can be difficult to classify. What some manufacturers consider to be a racing single others would call a recreational boat. For the purposes of this book, boats will be classified as wherries, recreational boats, or racing shells. A list of manufacturers is provided in the appendices.

BOATS

Wherries

The basic sculling boat, one that has been around since the watermen on the Thames first started racing each other to pick up customers, is the wherry. The wherry is an open boat somewhat shorter than other sculling boats, with a broad beam, sliding seat, and fixed riggers. Although it does not usually have a keel, it is stable due to its broad beam. In a relative sense, wherries are usually quite heavy, with some weighing in around 66 pounds. Many of the older wherries are wooden, although lately manufacturers have adopted fiberglass and plastic.

The Appledore Pod is a very stable, broad-beamed boat that novice scullers will feel comfortable in. Courtesy Martin Marine.

Wherries are excellent boats for beginners; they are stable, forgiving, and rugged. They are more comfortable to row in rough water than other sculling boats, and will help the novice sculler develop confidence and the ability to relax in a boat. Although wherries can be expensive, they tend to cost significantly less than other sculling boats.

Open-water boats, which share many characteristics with wherries, have additional features designed to meet the unique needs of open-water scullers. Since the boats may be rowed some distance from shore, the main considerations in this type are safety and seaworthiness. Open-water boats often have high gunwales and built-in flotation.

Recreational Boats

Recreational boats usually weigh more than 38 pounds and are up to 24 feet long, with a beam of 18 to 25 inches. They have bow and stern decks, an open cockpit, semi-adjustable riggers, and adjustable footstretchers with clogs. The hull design ranges from rounded to a flat-bottomed configuration, and rarely incorporates any kind of a keel, although some do have a fin.

Recreational boats are designed for the sculler interested in a responsive yet stable craft. Owners of these boats have often sculled for a time in a wherry and are looking for something a little more challenging, or they've rowed in college and want to continue rowing for exercise, or to race in the open water.

As more and more people have discovered the sport, this type of boat has become increasingly popular. It is much more affordable than a racing shell, and you can often find used recreational boats for sale.

The Maas Aero is often seen in long-distance races in the waters off California. Courtesy Maas Rowing Shells.

The Alden Ocean Shell, the most popular of the open-water boats. Courtesy Martin Marine.

Racing Shells

Racing shells are slender, light, responsive, high-performance boats used almost exclusively on protected lakes and rivers. They are much faster than recreational boats, and require a significantly higher skill level. Because they are more responsive and stiffer than other boats, they are also less forgiving of mistakes and much tougher to row in rough water.

A typical racing shell weighs 32 pounds or less, and is 25 to 28 feet long, with a 9 to 12 inch beam at the cockpit. It comes with track shoes sized to fit the sculler, fully adjustable riggers, and perhaps built-in wiring for an electronic strokemeter. Racing shells are very stiff, ensuring that the sculler's power is not lost in flexing the boat. Most of these shells are built with carbon fiber, epoxy, Kevlar, honeycomb, or other space-age materials.

While some manufacturers still build wooden boats, they are scarce. Although wooden shells may be as fast as their high-tech counterparts, most competitive scullers seem to have decided to go with the newer technology.

Racing shells are almost always custom-built to a sculler's specifications. Their prices match their performance; competitive scullers (and lots of not-very-competitive scullers) can easily spend upwards of $5,000 on a top-of-the-line shell. The boathouses of America are filled with beautiful boats that are rowed three or four times a year. They are a sizable investment, so make sure you are going to use it before you buy it.

If you do decide to purchase a racing shell, be prepared to wait several weeks to several months for a new boat. Since each boat is custom-made to the individual's specifications, most manufacturers require a minimum of two weeks from start to completion. Make sure you talk with the manufacturer about your present ability and skill level, what kind of shape you are in, how often and on what type of water (protected, windy, brackish) you plan to row, and what your goals are. Chances are the manufacturer will be able to make the boat even more useful to you if he knows a lot about you. For example, my shell's builder encouraged me to order an extra layer of carbon fiber in the bow to protect the hull from the logs common to the Potomac.

Racing singles
are built strictly
for speed on
relatively flat
water.

Boat Construction

Boats are made either from wood or from man-made materials. For some purists, wood is the only way to go. That's fine, but you have to realize that, generally speaking, wood requires more maintenance and more care than fiberglass. Several fine shells are still built of wood, including the Hudson and King. You may have a tough time obtaining one but if you want the real essence of the sport, it might be worth the effort.

Most wooden shells are made by bending very thin sheets of high-grade marine plywood, spruce, or cedar in a mold or around a frame. This bending process, which may be accomplished by a vacuum mold or moisture, naturally stresses the wood as it changes the natural shape of the material. Some manufacturers have developed different methods of molding the hulls that they claim result in a very strong, very durable shell with excellent longevity. To further strengthen the hull, some manufacturers are covering the outside with a thin layer of fiberglass. This additional step significantly adds to the strength of the hull and affords additional protection from the occasionally intrusive log or other navigational hazard.

Boats also are made of a variety of man-made materials, including fiberglass, Kevlar, carbon fiber, and honeycomb. The advantages of these materials lie in their excellent strength-to-weight ratios; pound for pound, Kevlar, a type of fiberglass, is stronger than steel. These materials can significantly increase rigidity and stiffness, characteristics that make a boat more efficient. A more flexible hull will be less efficient, as some of the sculler's power is lost in flexing instead of driving the boat forward.

The Kittery Skiff is a simple, inexpensive boat constructed of marine plywood. Courtesy Martin Marine.

There are many types of fiberglass, which is simply an open-weave fibrous cloth, much like rough-spun wool, that becomes rigid when combined with a liquid epoxy. Fiberglass is often used in wherries and recreational shells.

Kevlar is a very strong and very light fiberglass. It is used in bulletproof vests, car tires, and other applications where weight, bulk, and strength are important. Most "plastic" racing shells have some Kevlar in them.

Carbon fiber, or graphite, is used to strengthen and add rigidity to hulls and riggers. It is often woven into oars as well. The applications technology for carbon fiber is advancing very rapidly, with many of the techniques developed in the aerospace industry finding their way into shell manufacturing. It is used extensively in racing shells and may soon be used in recreational boats as well.

Honeycomb fiberglass, which looks just like you think it would, is used in the hull and solid decks of racing shells. By its nature, it provides rigidity without adding much weight. The honeycomb is usually sandwiched between two layers of Kevlar or other fiberglass.

Recently a British company developed an aluminum boat for the mass market. The model I had the opportunity to row was quite flexible and did not look too durable; I'd think twice before buying one.

Hull Design

Much has been made of the advantages, real or imagined, of one manufacturer's hull design over another's. Although some hull designs are inherently faster than others, the faster hulls are often less stable, so the increased speed is only available to those individuals who can scull well enough to take advantage of the faster hull design. Rough water can make some of the "fast" hulls feel like a mechanical bull. Again, try before you buy, and be realistic.

The power of computers and computer-aided design have resulted in some of the advances in hull design. These advances are all ways of decreasing the resistance the boat encounters, thus making them go faster with less effort.

Resistance is a function of both air and water creating friction as the boat moves. This friction cannot be summed up in a simple equation because the boat's speed increases and decreases during the stroke cycle as the sculler drives and recovers. Air accounts for a small percentage of the overall resistance. Ted Van Dusen of Composite Engineering has been working on lessening the effects of air resistance by modifying the shape of riggers and other components to decrease the amount of drag. Although the amount of friction created by air is not huge, it may become a factor in very close races, especially ones into a stiff headwind. Van Dusen's wing rigger is purported to reduce times for a 2000 meter race by 2 to 3 seconds, perhaps more in a headwind.

Interestingly, the depth of the water can have a significant effect on boat speed: Waves rebound off the bottom and can slow a boat. The shallower the water (down to 5 feet) and the slower the boat, the more significant the effect. There does not seem to be any measurable effect below 5 feet and at depths greater than 21 feet, the effects are virtually negligible. For example, if you're in a deep lane and your competition is in a 7-foot-deep lane, his time will be 2% slower (perhaps 9 seconds over 2000 meters) just from the depth differential.

Buying a Used Boat

If you're in the market for a boat, you may want to consider a used one for your first purchase. Used boats can be located through the USRA, your local boat club, or even the newspaper. There are scores of boats on the market; the only way to find out which one is right for you is to try as many as possible. You may be fortunate enough to have a dealer located in your area with boats available to test row. If not, you may wish to attend a sculling school to try a few models and get a little coaching at the same time. A list of sculling schools is included in the appendices.

If your sculling experience is limited to a couple of trips to a sculling school, start out with a recreational boat. You'll enjoy it and the sport much more than if you were to purchase a high-performance racing shell.

Van Dusen's aerodynamic wing rigger.

Before you hit the classifieds, do a little research and decide what your boat should be made of, how much you are willing to spend on it, the features you are looking for, how much refurbishing and repair work you are willing to undertake, and where you will store it. Another important factor is your size; boats are built for different weight classes, so be sure to look for one suitable for you. Finally, be honest with yourself and realistic in deciding what you would like to get from your sculling. Don't buy a particular model just because the national champs use it; buy the one that fits you best. The information provided below will give you a basic understanding of what to look for in a new boat as well as some questions to ask when investigating a previously-owned boat.

Condition of the Boat

Everyone has seen the classified ads that proclaim the advertised item is like new or was rarely used. Those descriptions probably apply more to racing shells than to any other type of sporting goods. Although a lot of exercise equipment is purchased with the best of intentions, those intentions often fall victim to tight schedules, family commitments, or other excuses. Because it is easier to rationalize your way out of sculling than most other athletic activities, many of the boats that go up for sale each year may not have been rowed more than 500 miles. If you look carefully, you can probably find one in near-new condition.

Hull

There are several things to be aware of when you get to the point of actually looking at a used boat you are considering buying. First, check the hull for indentations, bulges, obviously patched areas, and soft spots. Probably the best way to do this is to run your hand lightly along the hull. Another way is to look at the hull from various angles; light often hides imperfections from one angle and highlights them from another. At one time or another all boats will hit something floating in the water, so a patched area is not necessarily a cause for alarm. In fact, many riggers (people who fix boats) can repair extensively damaged hulls so the end result is a boat as strong and almost as light as it was when new. There are some pretty poor repair jobs out there as well, so look any repaired areas over carefully.

Significant bulges, dents, and soft spots in the hull will probably affect the performance of the boat and may indicate more serious problems. In all likelihood, these imperfections were caused by a poor repair job or defect in manufacturing. In a wooden hull, a soft spot or bulge may be caused by the delamination of the plywood or rot in the hull. Although this is rare, it does not bode well for the longevity of that boat. A bulge in a plastic boat may be the result of leaving the boat in direct sunlight for too long or from a poor repair job. Either way, examine the suspect area from both the inside and the outside to determine the extent of the problem.

Dents in either type of hull may not be important if they are small, and are probably the result of a minor encounter with a log. The same type of collision may cause scratches in the surface of the hull; if the scratches are deeper than the gelcoat on the first layer of glass or go into the wood, they should be repaired. Dents may also be caused by poor repair jobs and the other factors that produce bulges. Again, take your time, ask a lot of questions, and don't be afraid to turn around and drive home boatless if you aren't satisfied.

Fin

If the boat has a fin on the hull, examine it and the area around it carefully. Many boats have had their fins knocked loose or even completely off without any other harm caused. However, pay particular attention to the hull immediately in back of the fin. If the fin has been hit hard, it may have sliced back into the hull. This can be repaired, but is something to consider.

Some boats are designed to have the fin fall out upon impact, while others are designed so the fin is pushed up into the boat. Although both designs have their benefits, my preference is for the "disposable" fin. It is less likely to cause damage to the hull and requires less skill and time to repair. A design that incorporates an external sealed slot for the fin minimizes the chances of water entering the hull when the fin does come out. You will need to keep a spare fin or two handy or be prepared to pay the overnight express charges when the inevitable occurs.

Frame

Okay, you've looked the hull over carefully and it passes muster. Turn the boat over and examine it carefully from the bow to the stern. If possible, lift up part of the decking material and look over the frame inside the hull. Make sure the frame's struts are still bonded, tied, or otherwise fastened to the hull and each other in some logical fashion. You don't have to be an expert to tell if something has come loose; if all the other pieces that look like it are still attached and the one in question is off somewhere by itself, ask about it. Chances are the owner hasn't even noticed it yet.

These dimples may slow the boat since water cannot flow freely over the hull.

An externally-mounted fin. Notice also the carbon fiber woven into the hull.

A "throwaway" fin mounted in a slot in the hull.

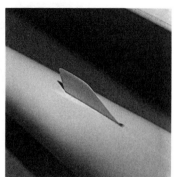

Deck

If the boat has a solid deck, check the deck just as you did the hull. Since the deck provides lateral stiffness, most solid-decked boats have little or no framing inside the hull. If the decking material isn't solid check it carefully. If it has tears or holes, count on replacing it immediately after you complete the purchase. A torn deck won't keep out water and may tear more when you are out sculling, leading to all kinds of problems, including sinking.

Cockpit

The cockpit and riggers are the last area to examine. Again, start your inspection from the bow. Check the rigidity of the washbox and make sure it is fastened to the deck in all the appropriate places. Tired scullers often accidently shove washboxes into boat racks, so give it a good going-over. There should be porthole arrangements in the bow and stern area of the cockpit. Open and close each one, making sure the porthole cover is attached to the boat with a cord. Next, examine the platform the tracks are fastened to. It should feel fairly solid, with no soft spots or cracks. Since this is the area you will be stepping on to, it should be in good shape. If the boat you are examining has an open cockpit, examine the supports under the tracks to make sure they are not cracked, missing nuts or bolts, or missing entirely.

Check the tracks themselves. They should be firmly fastened to the platform or supports and should be exactly parallel, both to each other and to the hull. Occasionally you'll come across a set of tracks that are set at an angle to the hull; avoid these arrangement at all costs. The tracks should be long enough to permit you to slide all the way forward until your shins are vertical, then all the way back until your legs are flat. If you are buying a racing shell, you may want to check to see if the tracks are adjustable fore and aft. This feature isn't crucial, but comes in handy in some rigging situations.

The frame of a wooden boat. Note also the repair in progress under the ropes. A plywood patch has been glued to the hull.

Check the porthole covers for a tight fit, open them and look into the hull in the bow and stern. There should be no water below the decks.

Footstretchers

After inspecting the tracks and surrounding area, take the footstretchers out of the boat and examine them. There are several methods of attaching the feet to the boat; the basic Velcro strap across the arch; the clog, an open-toed leather sandal arrangement with a metal heel cup; and the running or track shoe. It's a good idea to install a pair of your old running shoes to give you a custom fit. If the footstretchers are of the non-shoe variety, make sure the device for holding the foot in the footstretcher is in good shape and firmly attached to the sole.

In most racing shells and recreational boats, the sole of the footstretcher attaches to the top bar and the bottom bar with two bolts or screws connecting each sole to each bar. Make sure the soles are not attached at an uncomfortable angle, either too steep or too wide at the top.

Next look at the mechanism for attaching the footstretcher to the hull. It should be firmly attached to the hull, with no play at all in the attachment. There are usually three plates the stretcher is attached to: one on each side and one on the keel. Check all of them. Install the stretcher in several different sets of holes to make sure the bolts and holes line up correctly.

Riggers

The riggers are the last part of the boat to check. First, examine the attachment points where the riggers are bolted to the hull. There should be no play in the rigger when it is bolted to the boat, and it should bolt on without having to be forced into place. If the riggers are metal, check the joints for cracks or signs of repair. If they are carbon fiber or fiberglass, look closely for any scratches or dings in the struts. When carbon fiber fails, it does so instantly, catastrophically, and expensively; so be thorough.

A well-worn rigger. The welds are neatly done but signal a great deal of use.

Check the oarlocks and the pins or metal bolts the oarlocks swivel on. They should swivel freely from side to side. Examine the oarlocks for signs of excessive wear or twisting. If they have tape wrapped around the top or bottom, the oarlocks are probably not correctly set to the pitch of the oars. Ask the owner how to adjust the pitch or height of the oarlocks; if the answer involves bending anything or using tape or raising one side of the rigger, beware: This type of oarlock can be quite a bit of work.

While this survey is important, it is only part of the information on which to base the "buy/no buy" decision. If at all possible, take the boat out for a row. You don't have to go very far, a couple of miles should give you a good feel for the handling and stability of a boat. The boat may be rigged differently from the boat you're used to; try to pay attention to the way the boat glides on the recovery, the way it handles rough water, and the way it responds to hard pulling. Those indications will go a long way toward telling you if this is the right boat for you.

Once you've purchased a used boat, you may be able to get an owner's manual from the manufacturer if you call and ask very nicely. The people who build rowing equipment almost always row themselves, so the manuals are pretty good and address most of the questions you will want to have answered. If you don't understand something or have a question, call the manufacturer and ask.

Sculls

The traditional scull or sculling oar is wood with a spoon-shaped blade and is 298 centimeters long, or about 12 feet. The handle is covered with a smooth or textured soft rubber grip. This traditional scull has been replaced in many oar racks by the newer composite sculls. Although wood sculls are aesthetically more pleasing, they are definitely heavier and require more maintenance. If you are in the market for sculls, avoid wood unless you really like it for aesthetic reasons. Some scullers like the heavier feel of wood; it helps to balance the boat. If that is true in your case, order a pair of composite oars and ask the manufacturer to put a little extra weight in the blade end of the shaft. The lighter the oar, the less energy you have to expend in moving it about.

A lot of progress has been made recently in the design and construction of composite oars. The Driessigacker brothers and their associates at Concept II have been very influential in this effort, and continue to experiment with new designs and materials.

In 1987 Concept II began producing sculls weighing in at just under 3 pounds. These sculls are 25 percent lighter than most composite sculls, which in turn are significantly lighter than wooden ones. While not appropriate for novice scullers since they do little to help balance the boat, they do seem to help get the hands out of bow a little quicker and save a little energy. Other manufacturers are also producing light, composite sculls. Check with the USRA for a list of suppliers.

The "delta" blade is another Concept II innovation. Compared with the standard blade, the delta is more triangular and is wider at the tip. According to Judy Geer of Concept II, this shape gives a lighter feel at the catch and a heavier feel through the middle of the drive. The shift of surface area out toward the tip of the blade accomplishes this by increasing the lift of the oar at the catch and increasing drag when the oar is perpendicular to the boat.

The delta blade is supposed to be more appropriate for recreational and slower racing boats, such as the single and double. It may be slightly more difficult to clear the water with the delta since the tip of the blade is pretty wide. Concept II does offer a modified delta which looks like a standard blade on the bottom with a delta blade on top. This may alleviate any problems associated with the release. Interestingly, the delta resembles the shapes of blades from the 1950s. The more things change....

When purchasing oars you should get them with zero pitch at the blade. This will make it easier to rig your boat and will also make it more likely that your oars will be compatible with someone else's boat if you happen to borrow it or decide to go out in a double.

The stiffness of the oar is also important. Experienced and well-conditioned scullers are better off with a stiffer oar, novices with a less-stiff oar. The faster you are going the less you want the oar to bend. If the oar has to unbend at the release, it may reduce the smoothness of the release.

While almost all sculls are 298 centimeters, you may be better off with 296s if you're somewhat short on upper body strength to start. Only the very biggest and very strongest scullers will need sculls longer than 298 centimeters, so try not to kid yourself.

Finally, your sculls should have matching balance points. When you balance them on your finger, the balance points must be within an inch of each other or they will feel different. In addition, the closer the balance point is to the oarlock, the lighter the oar will feel as you scull.

If you are in the market for a new pair of sculls, call up a few of the suppliers, tell them what you are looking for and why and ask them what they think. Since these folks are some of the only people able to actually make a living from sculling, they really do know their stuff and are always willing to share information and suggestions.

Chapter Four

Rigging

igging is the process of setting up your boat so you can comfortably, efficiently, and effectively scull. Some scullers seem to make rigging needlessly complicated—they spend hours, days, even whole seasons trying to find just the right settings for their boat. These types forget the immortal words of George Pocock, who once said, "The three Rs of rowing are not rigging, rigging, rigging, but rowing, rowing, rowing." Couldn't agree with you more, George.

Rigging can not help a slow sculler become fast any more than a more expensive set of sculls will make him a better sculler. Within limits, the correct rig is a personal thing; some scullers like the handles a bit higher than others, some want a little more overlap on the crossover, others like their footstretchers angled just a bit more than the standard configuration. You will find the best configuration for yourself by trial and error, but don't try too much. If you find a rig that's comfortable and effective, stop right there.

Some scullers also vary their rig with the season. A heavier load in the off-season ostensibly allows the sculler to hang on the oars a bit more. Perhaps, but a heavier load also increases your chances of injury and does not replicate the stresses you will experience when you are sculling at a higher rating.

Your stroke should be quick and deft as well as explosive and powerful. If you've made it harder to pull the oars through the water by increasing the load significantly, you will slow down the entire stroke, including the initial part of the drive and the release. This decrease in quickness and speed may remove some of the finesse and deftness from your sculling, making you a puller instead of a sculler. Besides, it is just plain easier to rig the boat and leave it than to constantly screw around with it. Spend your rigging time sculling and you'll see a better return on your investment.

There are basically two types of sculling boats, those with adjustable rigging and those with fixed rigging. Even some of the fixed rigging can be adjusted. Almost all sculling boats built in the last few years have adjustable rigging, although some may be more adjustable than others. "Fully adjustable" includes the pitch of the oarlock, both fore-and-aft and lateral; span, or distance between the oarlocks; height of the oarlocks; and the fore-and-aft position of the seat tracks.

There are a few rules of thumb regarding rigging a sculling boat. In the U.S. the boat is set up to allow enough clearance for the left hand to comfortably cross over the right. Some Europeans do the opposite (right over left) and some simply lead one hand in front of the other; so the rule of thumb depends on whose thumb is ruling. Other guidelines, such as the height of the heels relative to the tracks and the most appropriate oar length, have been determined as a result of much trial and error by thousands of scullers. It will be the rare sculler who finds he is so unique that a setting outside of the parameters described below is best.

Rigging is just like any other part of your sculling. If you are to improve, you must know where you are starting from and you must be able to identify the changes you have made so you can assess their impact. Once you have rigged your boat, record all measurements in your logbook. Then, whenever you make a change, record the change as well. Make only one change at a time or you'll get all confused. Finally, you should periodically measure things to make sure the rig hasn't slipped. I once discovered the day before the Nationals that my pitch had drastically changed.

There are five important considerations when rigging a shell. These include:

- adjusting the footstretchers to accommodate leg length;
- height of the work (oarlocks);
- position of the seat relative to the oarlocks;
- pitch of the blade; and
- load, which is a function of the distance between the oarlocks (also known as spread or span) and the position of the button or collar on the oar

FOOTSTRETCHER ADJUSTMENT

We covered the basics of adjusting footstretchers in Chapter 1. Actually it's not quite that simple. Footstretcher adjustment affects and is affected by the load and height of the work. Therefore, if you change either one of these measurements, you may have to modify your stretcher position if the oar handles jab you in the stomach

The spread can be adjusted by placing blocks between the rigger and the gunwale; height can be changed with shims under the lower or upper bolts on the rigger; pitch changed by bending the rigger.

One of the more-adjustable oarlocks on the market.

or are too far away from you at the finish. When you change the load, check the stretcher position by sitting at the finish with your hands drawn in and the blades buried. Your thumbs (over the ends of the oar handles) will just brush your shirt if the footstretchers are set correctly.

The other footstretcher measurements you should be aware of include the horizontal angle of the footstretcher and the opening angle between the feet. The horizontal angle should be around 45 degrees for men and 42 degrees for women. Neither of these numbers is absolute. If you have too much angle, the heels will lift up as you slide up to the catch, reducing your ability to drive at the catch. Conversely, too little angle and you will have trouble straightening out your legs.

The opening angle of the feet should be 15 to 25 degrees. Too much and your knees will be spread out too far at the catch. Too little angle may cause biomechanical problems as your legs are forced to move in an unnatural pattern. In addition, if the angle is too tight, you will find yourself driving off the outside of your foot.

HEIGHT OF WORK

The height of the work (work is defined for our purposes as the fulcrum, or more precisely the bottom of the inside of the oarlock) is also a simple measurement. The starboard oarlock should be 1/8 to 1/4 inch (10mm to 20mm) higher than the port to allow for the crossover. The port oarlock should be approximately 10 inches (240mm) above the water (when you are sitting in the boat) and 7 inches (170mm) above the gunwale. A more common way of measuring the height is the distance from the seat to the bottom of the oarlock. Simply slide the seat all the way toward the stern and measure the distance from the seat to the top of the gunwale. Using a simple straightedge or a rigging stick (make sure it really is straight), measure the distance from the gunwale to the bottom of the inside of the oarlock and add the distances together. A normal measurement is 5 inches (135mm), although you may want it a little higher if you scull in rough water or have large thighs that demand more room to clear the oar handles at the finish. Novices also seem to have more success with a slightly higher rig, although you should try to lower the height as you improve.

If your work is too high, the leg drive's effectiveness at the catch will be hampered and you will be likely to wash out at the finish. Conversely, insufficient height will result in furrows dug into the tops of your thighs by your fingernails as you try to get the hands out on the recovery. You will also batter your knees about if you can't get the handles over them on the recovery.

SEAT POSITION

The fore-and-aft position of the seat (at the catch) relative to the oarlocks gives you the measurement known as the "distance through the pin." The through-the-pin measurement affects the catch and release angle; too much distance through-the-pin and you pinch the boat at the catch, too little and the boat is pinched at the release. Pinching the boat refers to a position of the blades in the water such that

Height of work: Slide the seat all the way toward the stern and measure the distance from the seat to the top of the gunwale using a straightedge. . .

. . . Then measure the distance from the gunwale to the bottom of the inside of the oarlock and add the two distances together.

the direction of force exerted by the blades is at an acute angle relative to the boat. This acute angle means that the force exerted by the blades on the water "pinches" the hull.

The angles also are affected by the span and the load on the oars. The tighter the span and more load on the oars, the longer your stroke. Too tight a span, too heavy a load, and you'll be pinching the boat. This is another reason to be cautious and only make one rigging change at a time. If you load the blades up, move the pins in, and move the tracks toward the stern, you will change the entire feel of the boat. If you do decide to make wholesale changes, measure everything before and after.

Distance through-the-pin is a relatively simple measurement to make. Roll the seat all the way up toward the stern. Next, place your rigging stick or other straightedge on top of the pins and measure the distance from the center of the pin to the front of the seat. An appropriate measurement might be 1 to 2 inches (2 to 4 centimeters), but the best way to figure out where you should be is to scull at various ratings and pressures and watch how far forward your seat rolls. The wheels on the seat should come to within a half-inch of your front stops.

BLADE PITCH

Pitch is the most popular aspect of rigging. It has to do with the pitch, or angle, of the blade as it enters and proceeds through the water. Correct pitch ensures that your blade is always solidly buried in the water and you can pull effectively all the

Unless you're noticeably too long or too short at the catch, leave the through-the-pin where it is.

way through the stroke. You should be aware that pitch is a function of the pitch of the oar itself as well as the oarlock. Nowadays most sculls are built with zero degrees of pitch so all pitch adjustment is done by altering the pitch of the oarlock.

There are a couple ways of determining pitch. Both must be done on land. To measure the total pitch, place the oar in the oarlock and hold it firmly against the pin while holding the boat level, both fore-and-aft and port-to-starboard. Using a pitchmeter, measure the pitch of the blade at the catch, middle of the drive, and finish. Most scullers are comfortable with a catch pitch of 6 or 7 degrees and a release pitch around 4 degrees. This decrease in pitch makes it easier to get the blades out of the water at the finish. The change in pitch during the pull-through is determined by the lateral, or sideways, pitch of the oarlock. The more lateral pitch, the more the pitch of the blade will change on the pull-through. A standard setting is 1.5 degrees outward pitch.

The second way to determine pitch is to measure the pitch of the oarlock and the pitch of the blade separately, then add the two figures together. Although most of the composite (fiberglass and related materials) oars available come with zero pitch, they can twist over time and with heavy use, so it pays to measure the blade pitch every few months. Twisting is more of a problem with wooden sculls.

To measure the pitch of the oarlock, simply level the boat fore-and-aft and port-to-starboard and measure the pitch of the oarlock's vertical face parallel to the pin. A cautionary note: Make sure the pitchmeter is flush against the back of the oarlock and make sure you check the pitch at the catch, middle, and finish. Blade pitch is easily determined by placing the oar over the ground with the flat part of the button on a level block. Use your pitchmeter on the tip of the blade.

Too much pitch will cause you to wash out, and too little causes the blade to knife, or sink into the water. Again, pitch doesn't have to be perfect to the tenth of a degree and your preferred pitch may be different from the measurement preferred by another sculler. Go with what feels right.

Use a small level to ensure the boat is on an even keel when you wish to measure pitch.

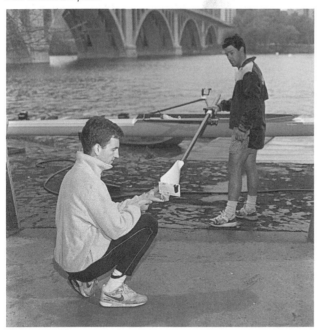

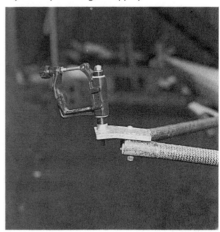

A Concept II oarlock showing lateral pitch. The fore-and-aft pitch is easily and permanently adjusted by inserting the appropriate shim.

LOAD

The load on the oars determines how much effort you have to exert to get the blades through the water. Load is another name for leverage and is determined by changing the relationship of the lever, or scull, and the fulcrum, or pin. By decreasing the span and/or decreasing the inboard length of the oar (the part of the oar from the handle to the button, or collar), you decrease the amount of leverage you have. If you increase the span and/or inboard, you increase your leverage. Too much load (not enough leverage) and your stroke will be slow and sluggish; it may also increase your chances of injury. Too little load (too much leverage) and you will be windmilling through the water.

Of all rigging measurements, load is the most individual. For example, if you like to row at a high rate, you'll want a lighter load than someone who prefers to grind it out at a low rate. You should do a little experimenting with your load adjustment each year, preferably in the fall unless you get a new boat in the spring. This is the one aspect of rigging where you will occasionally change two settings at the same time: the load on the oar (affected by moving the button) and the span (the distance between the pins). You may want to increase or decrease the load if you'll be racing into a headwind or with a tailwind.

There are several rules of thumb pertaining to load. First, the length of the inboard lever (oar measured from the face of the button to the end of the handle) should be 4 to 6 1/2 inches (110mm to 180mm) longer than the span to allow for crossover. Second, a 1 1/2-inch (40mm) change in the load on the oar corresponds to a 1/2-inch (10mm) change in the span. Finally, when you change the span, the height of the work also changes by an 8:1 ratio. To accommodate this factor most of the riggers are designed so the strut the pin is attached to slopes toward the water, effectively eliminating the change in the height of the work due to a change in span.

You can also vary the resistance on the oars by varying the position of the button, which determines the fulcrum. If you've purchased a new boat, oars, or both, the manufacturer will usually include a manual illustrating the technique for rigging that particular boat or oar. In most cases the manufacturer will also deliver the boat set up to your specifications. Check it anyway to make sure.

Always record your rigging adjustments and measurements in your logbook. Although the correct measurements may take a little time to determine, if you're patient and don't try to do too much too fast, you should be able to get your boat set up in a month or two. Once that is done all you have to do is perhaps move the button a bit to allow for the effects of a headwind or tailwind. Do make an effort to measure everything every six weeks, or whenever something just feels wrong. This should enable you to catch any slippage before it gets too severe.

The following chart will give you a few parameters you may want to consider when rigging your boat. Again, set your boat up for you. Don't use an Olympic sculler's rigging measurements unless you are in that class.

COMMON RIGGING MEASUREMENTS

Class	Oar length	Inboard	Spread
Recreational women	296	86 – 89	161 – 164
Light women	296	88 – 89	161 – 163
Women	296/298	87 – 88	160 – 163
Recreational men	296/298	84 – 89	158 – 165
Light men	298	86 – 87	160 – 163
Men	298/300	84 – 87	157 – 160

All measurements are in centimeters.

Follow the instructions that came with the pitchmeter carefully, and hold it snug against the pin.

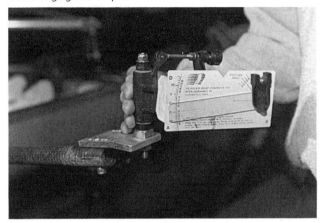

Measure the total span and the distance from the keel to each oarlock to ensure they are equal. Simply determine the width of the boat at the gunwales, divide by two, and add that to the distance from the gunwale to the oarlock.

To set the inboard, first measure, change the button, and then remeasure to make sure you got it right. . .

. . . Then all you have to do is match the measured oar to the others you wish to set. This is very helpful when rigging a double or a quad.

Chapter Five

Advanced Technique

 culling correctly is not an attainable goal, it is a process with no end. Good technique is hard to learn and easily forgotten. After sculling for ten years I find myself making mistakes I thought were corrected eight years ago. Undoubtedly your experience will be similar; you'll fix one flaw only to find another cropping up. Don't despair, this is simply the nature of the sport.

Sculling looks easy only when done very well because it is actually a very complex series of movements that must be carefully orchestrated if a correct stroke is to result. This orchestration must then be repeated for the next stroke and each stroke after that. The complicated nature of this movement ensures that at any one time something is flawed; there is no perfect stroke. Some scullers find great satisfaction in this quest alone, others find it quite frustrating.

Frank Cunningham, a highly respected sculling coach in Seattle, has compared the single boat to a prima donna, constantly demanding attention. An apt analogy, and one with which most scullers would agree. Sculling well in a single is not a mindless pursuit, but rather one that requires a continuous focus on the task at hand if you are to improve.

You will find times when you are sculling along fairly well with your head in the ozone; this does not contradict the image of the boat as an unforgiving taskmaster. These episodes are fleeting. You are not improving your sculling when you are out for a mindless row and, upon returning to the dock, may actually find you have acquired new flaws in your technique or have slipped back into old, bad habits. Guard against mindless rows because they will inevitably lead to a degeneration in your skill level. Every now and again it may be nice to go out for a nature paddle, but a constant diet of them will slow you down.

Since the early days when every outing was new and unusual you've learned quite a bit about sculling itself. You have learned to keep your blades off the water, perhaps even at full pressure. Chances are you have tested yourself against some of your friends on the river. You may even be feeling confident. If so, it's time to make the transition from learning about sculling to learning how to scull.

MEMORY

At least half of your success will be attributable to your mental ability. You must be able to learn how to scull and scull well under various conditions, including the intense pressure of competition. For some reason few scullers take the time to learn how to train the mind or even to learn what impact the mind has on their sculling. Perhaps it is because people can admit to a physical weakness more readily than to a mental weakness, or perhaps because there is little glamour in mental training. Regardless of their reasoning, scullers who ignore mental training would be far better off if they cut back on their physiological conditioning and spent that time on mental training.

There are three types of memory you use when you are learning to scull: the short-term sensory store, short-term memory, and long-term memory. Everyone has these three types of memory and the memory capacity for all adults is about the same. The difference between people is how they use their memory abilities.

Short-term Sensory Store

The short-term sensory store does exactly what its name implies: it receives and holds massive amounts of sensory input from the eyes, ears, limb receptors, and other sensory organs. It can hold a huge amount of raw data, but only raw data and only for a short time. Because the short-term sensory store is constantly being bombarded with new sensory input, raw data remain in the store for one second at the outside. This sensory store acts as a data collection tool for the next highest memory function, the short-term memory. However, only a tiny fraction of the data collected can be passed on to the short-term memory, at most six to eight specific items. To better understand the short-term sensory store, think of quickly pouring a lot of water into a jug using a funnel with a large mouth and very small spout. Most of the water would overflow the funnel, but a little will make it through the small spout into the jug, or short-term memory. The rest is lost. The trick is to be able to select what gets into your short-term memory.

Short-term Memory

If you are to learn, you must be able to program your short-term memory to accept only the important bits of data from your short-term sensory store. If random bits of data flood into your brain, you will be overflowing with relevant and irrelevant information. You will be unable to make any decisions, conscious or unconscious, or perform any movements except those triggered by panic. This ability to program your memory, or to focus, is vital to your success, and more importantly your ultimate enjoyment of the sport.

Once the few bits of data are in the short-term memory, they will stay there for at most sixty seconds. It might be helpful to think of the short-term memory as the present experience. This information, or present experience, is combined with other bits of sensory information as it continues to come in from the short-term sensory store and compared with images stored in the third type of memory, the long-term memory. This comparison enables you to determine if your actions are the correct ones and to identify the alterations necessary to make your stroke more closely resemble the correct image.

Long-term Memory

The long-term memory, a repository of past experience, stores selected, learned motor skills forever. However, unless you are careful, you can "forget" certain motor skills if very similar ones are learned, or if they weren't practiced enough when they were first acquired.

When the comparison between your present experience and long-term memory is made, you are able to use information to decide which of your learned motor skills you will select to initiate a movement. Producing the correct movement is dependent on selecting the right short-term sensory input from the short-term sensory store, comparing it with other immediate inputs held in the short-term memory to identify a pattern, comparing that pattern with what you have experienced in the past, and selecting the appropriate motor program from your long-term memory's inventory of learned movements.

Learning the "appropriate motor program" is a gradual process. A trace of a new movement is loaded into the long-term memory. Each subsequent movement builds on that memory, strengthening it, and slightly modifying it until what you hope is the correct movement is "set" in the long-term memory.

This is why mindless sculling can be so dangerous. Even if you are only sculling a few miles without thinking, your body is actually learning to perform movements. If these are the wrong movements, you have not only wasted the time you were sculling in the ozone, but you now have to take the time to correct the mistakes you've ingrained into your memory.

LEARNING

There are three stages of learning: cognitive, associative, and automatic.

Cognitive Stage

In the cognitive stage, you are learning what to do instead of how to do it. You have to think about each movement, and you aren't sure which movements are the right ones. You are starting to build an image of correctness, a picture in your mind of what a sculling stroke should look like. This image can be built from books, films, coaching and instruction, and or by watching other scullers.

Associative Stage

During the associative stage, you begin to learn how to scull. You get out on the water and start figuring out what works for you and what doesn't. During this phase of learning you'll find yourself observing others and learning from them; you start to focus on different components of the sculling stroke as you become aware of its subtleties. This understanding also leads to a whole series of "light bulb over the head" experiences as you begin to correctly perform various parts of the stroke yourself and things start to make sense.

Automatic Stage

In the final stage of learning, the automatic phase, the movements comprising the skills have been practiced so often that they become automatic; you don't have to think about them because you have set them in your memory.

Throughout this learning process, you have to have some frame of reference that will enable you to identify your mistakes by giving you something to compare yourself to. This frame of reference is called the "knowledge of results."

KNOWLEDGE OF RESULTS

Olympic athletes occasionally have the benefit of computerized motion analysis, a very precise method of tracking an athlete's motions while he performs. The analysis enables the athlete to compare his motion with the perfect model and then identify any variations. On a basic level, computerized motion analysis simply provides the athlete with a highly accurate and precise knowledge of results.

If you cannot afford real motion analysis, there is an alternative that may be more suited to your budget. Videotaping can help you understand what you're doing in a boat, and watching tapes of highly-skilled scullers will give you a better picture of the ideal motion. It is one thing for someone to tell you that you are rushing the slide, but often you don't really understand the problem until you see it for yourself and compare it to an ideal. This understanding is crucial if you're to improve.

Using the principle of knowledge of results to improve your technique is pretty straightforward. First, you must create in your mind a precise picture of a good sculling stroke. You may get the basis for this picture from watching good scullers, looking at slow-motion videotape, or examining drawings or photos. Next, when you are out sculling, focus on one specific aspect of your stroke and very precisely identify how it differs from the ideal model you have in your mind. Since you'll want to give yourself time to focus on the differences, pause between each stroke, understand what was correct about the last stroke, why, and what was incorrect and why. You may want to pause every second, third, or tenth stroke as you get the problem corrected.

This pause will enable you to compare your sensory data with the picture stored in your long-term memory. The result will be a slightly modified action during the next stroke, which will again be compared to the ideal stroke. This process, a series of minute changes and improvements, continues until you are satisfied your stroke precisely mimics the ideal picture, as you see it in your mind. As you make technical improvements, the motion becomes set in your memory through continuous, conscious repetition until it becomes automatic. Unless you are very talented, your stroke will never be flawless, so get used to this process.

The principles outlined above show not only that practice makes perfect, but that right practice makes perfect. You have to know what perfect is and you have to focus your mind to ensure the short-term sensory store picks up the data you need to evaluate your performance, and only those data. This focus is not possible if you are not concentrating on the task at hand. Remember, mindless rows will set you back by implanting poor technique and not enhancing good technique.

VISUALIZATION

Visualization is a powerful tool you can use to make the most of your water time. It is also something that many scullers just don't make the time for; not because they have more important things to do but because they fail to understand the extent to which the mind and mental training dictate their performance.

Visualization works because the brain does not distinguish between actually physically performing a stroke, an "external" experience, and creating a mental, or "internal," picture of this performance. In fact, when you become adept at visualizing certain situations you will find the body reacts as if it were actually performing the actions you are visualizing. For example, if you are sitting in your Barca-lounger at home and visualize a race right before the start, you will find that your heart rate increases, legs tense, breathing quickens, and butterflies invade your stomach. Not the physiological activity one normally associates with Barca-lounging, but the brain has transported the body out of the TV room and into a racing shell.

There are two functions served by visualization. The first is to test-run motor programs to obtain a positive transfer of skills. In other words, to make a mental image of the way you should row and make that a reality in your actual physical performance.

Visualization's second function helps you to prepare for different situations you may encounter while sculling. Mental imagery techniques enable you to anticipate possible situations that may cause you anxiety or stress. In turn, this anxiety or stress can generate a host of unwanted and potentially damaging physical and mental reactions. Using mental imagery to anticipate those situations and to program your response will help you to overcome anxiety and stress by avoiding them altogether. If you think through your reaction to a mid-race crab before the race begins, you will be much better equipped to handle a crab during the race. You will also be less likely to panic, tighten up, or otherwise lose speed if you are well prepared. In short, you are not adequately preparing yourself if you do not use imagery techniques as part of your daily training ritual.

There are three different types of visualization techniques and each is used for a different purpose. The first technique is modeling, which is used to create a mental picture of the ideal state, such as the perfect catch. Mental rehearsal, the second visualization technique, is used for simulating races or other important situations. The third technique is reframing, or corrective visualization; you'll find it very helpful in understanding what you are doing wrong and how to make it right.

Your preparations for visualization should always be the same; the more consistent you are, the easier it will be for you to get into your visualization mode. The first step is to get into a comfortable position and focus on your breathing, excluding all external stimuli. When you have relaxed and are focusing well, you are ready to begin the actual visualization part of the session.

One relaxation technique used by some scullers is quite similar to the breathing techniques used in the martial arts. To begin the technique, lie down or seat yourself comfortably. Then, for two or three seconds firmly press the index and middle fingers of either hand into the abdomen, about an inch or so below the navel. As soon as you stop pressing the spot, begin a series of five deep, measured breaths. Count to five as you inhale, hold the breath for five counts, and slowly exhale, again over a count of five. Feel the spot you were pressing on move in when you exhale and out when you inhale.

Concentrate on the spot and the counting, exclude other thoughts from your mind, and feel your entire body slowly sinking into the chair. If you aren't relaxed and focused after the fifth breath, don't be too concerned. Visualization, like sculling, takes practice.

Modeling

You can use modeling whether you are just learning to scull or just working on a specific aspect of the stroke. By implanting a precise picture of the correct position, movement, or feeling in your mind, you will have a much better understanding of the action.

Before you begin your modeling session, you will need to precisely identify the ideal state and create a picture of it in your mind. You can look at pictures or videos of the desired action or perhaps watch other scullers. If possible, scull in a team boat behind a sculler with superior technique. After you have a clear picture of what you want to model in your sculling, begin the session.

When you are relaxed and focused, bring the model picture into your mind's eye as if it were a TV screen. Watch the picture closely, examining each part of the action intently. See the action performed perfectly, exactly copying the image you stored in your mind down to such detail as the motion of waves against the hull. Once you can see the image clearly, bring yourself into the picture by placing yourself next to the ideal sculler in your mind, as if you were sculling in a double. Put yourself into the bow seat and watch yourself sculling precisely with the sculler in the stern seat who is sculling perfectly.

If you are using still pictures or drawings, it's critical to imagine (and thereby incorporate) movement into the pictures as they are copied into your mind. The best way to use still pictures is to place them in series and look at them in sequence. If you don't copy them into your mind as moving pictures in correct sequence, the process won't be very useful.

Finally, make the experience physical by tensing and relaxing your legs, back, and arms as you watch yourself scull. Be careful to use your muscles in the same sequence you do when you are in the boat. Remember, the brain thinks you are actually out sculling, so you want to incorporate the physical sensations into the image as well to build a complete mental picture of the correct action you are seeking.

Modeling is best used just before you scull. Take a few minutes to complete a session, focusing on the specific part of the stroke you want to improve or change. Visualization takes at most ten minutes when you start the practice; with experience you can complete an entire modeling session in two or three minutes.

Don't make the mistake of skipping mental training in favor of an extra mile or two on the water; mental training is just as important as the day's physical workout.

Mental Rehearsal

The second type of visualization is mental rehearsal or, technically speaking, the simulation or mental exercise of an event designed to emulate that event. You can use mental rehearsal to go through the training program for that day or to simulate race conditions.

The key is to focus on precisely what you want to work on that day. See the action clearly in your mind's eye, perhaps in slow motion, and feel the sensations by incorporating physical sensations into the visualization. Mental rehearsal is especially helpful in setting a race plan in your mind. It is easy to get distracted during a race, especially if you don't have a race plan embedded in your brain.

To use this technique, begin concentrating on your sculling after you are relaxed and focused. Use the breathing technique described earlier. Start the rehearsal with the push away from the dock and proceed through your warm-up. If you're rehearsing a race, see that race clearly in your mind's eye. Pay particular attention to the key segments: the start, the settle, and the middle part of the race. Feel the boat during this exercise; feel yourself sculling smoothly and effectively throughout the entire race. You will find this imagery is most effective if you see the entire boat and the entire workout or race several times; this repetition helps set the image in your mind.

You don't have to spend a lot of time at this; a few minutes should be sufficient.

Reframing

Reframing is a more specific type of visualization used to change bad habits you've developed, whether in your technique, ability to focus during a practice, or another aspect of your sculling. Too many scullers denigrate themselves for perceived weaknesses or flaws instead of working with a positive attitude to solve the problem. This negative attitude contributes to the problem as you become tense and further entrench the error in your nervous system.

Reframing is a positive way to understand a flaw and correct it using positive imagery. To use this technique, prepare yourself as you did for the other types of imagery. When you are relaxed and focused, concentrate on a past time when your sculling was flawed and then, on the steps you took to correct those flaws. Next, establish a picture of yourself sculling perfectly and a picture of yourself sculling today. You'll see the differences between the two pictures; the flaws in your technique as compared to the ideal picture.

Make the picture of your flawed sculling mimic the ideal; see the changes that are made as your present style becomes perfect and focus on those changes. As you mentally change your style, focus on the ideal sculling stroke and hold it in your mind as the picture on which to focus.

Most of the scullers I know are obsessive-compulsive types who get frustrated with visualization because they can't get it to work the first time they try it. Don't discard visualization because it's difficult to do when you first try it; remember how impossible sculling was the first time you got into a boat. Used effectively, these techniques can help you make improvements quickly and avoid the plateaus when you just can't seem to go any faster or scull any better. As for the time involved, remember that the typical human brain thinks at the rate of approximately 600 words per second. With practice, your mental training will be over quickly but the benefits for your sculling won't be.

TECHNICAL CONSIDERATIONS

Good sculling is made up of two very basic ideas; using your energy efficiently and allowing the boat to work for you. Think about the sculling motion for a minute. It requires you to move the bulk of your weight back and forth in the boat, pitching the shell first down at the bow at the catch, and then down at the stern. This pitching motion is inherently inefficient because it causes the boat to move through its designed waterline.

To get an idea of the effect of this pitching, sit in your boat with your legs flat, swing your back back-and-forth and watch the waves emanating from the hull. These waves are identical, albeit smaller, to the waves you create when you use the slide. Because the boat is most efficient when it is moving level in the water, or along its designed waterline, you want to minimize the pitching of the hull.

The best way to do this is to row connected and to row quiet. Rowing connected means keeping pressure on the oar handles and the footstretchers all the way through the drive; rowing quiet means a smooth catch, perfectly timed to enter the water at the right time with minimal splash, minimal noise, and a fast, smooth release causing little disturbance in the water. Easily stated, difficult to make a reality.

Rowing Connected

Rowing connected is also known as hanging on the oars, suspending the body between the handles and the stretchers, driving up and back, or sculling "light in the seat." It requires you to suspend your body weight from the oar handles as you drive. The weight is supported by the blades pressing against the water while your feet are pressing against the stretchers. This gets your mass out of the boat and lifts the boat out of the water, reducing the wetted-surface area and thus, drag.

Some scullers understand this concept better when they think of getting their weight out of the seat. Visualize yourself sitting in the sculling position with your feet against a wall, holding on to a bar attached to the wall with your rear end an inch or two off the ground. This feeling of weight suspended from the hands and feet is the feeling you are striving for in the boat.

Rowing connected involves keeping your weight on the oar handles through-out the drive. To start to get the right feeling, scull at light pressure with your feet out. Feel the oar handles pressing into your fingers from the instant they enter the water at the catch all the way to the release. Keep your weight on your footstretchers all the way through as well.

The key part of the drill is the point where the back moves through the perpendicular; you have to keep the pressure on by increasing the arm draw from there on into the finish. When you start getting this right, you'll see that everything finishes at the same time: your arm draw is complete, your legs go down, your back completes the pull-through. You'll find that the speed of the hands moving away from the body at the release has greatly increased without any conscious effort on your part.

Congratulations, you're starting to row connected.

If you're having trouble finding the right feeling, look at your blades just as they exit the water at the release. If you are pulling all the way through the stroke as you

At the catch, drive up and back so that your rear end lifts ever so slightly off the seat. This forces you to hang on the oars.

should, the blades will come out of the middle of the puddle; if not, the puddle will be past the blade before the blade is out of the water. The blade may also be continuing its movement toward the stern after it exits the water. If this is happening to you, it shows you are not keeping pressure all the way into the finish and the blades are going slower than the boat at the release, dragging out of the water and slowing you down.

Once you're able to finish the stroke off normally, sculling with the feet out, start adding pressure. More than likely the added pressure will make the drill easier as it forces the heels down into the stretcher. With practice, the finish will become more fluid and controlled and the effect of your weight coming off the oar handles at the release will be minimized as well.

When you place your feet in the stretchers after sculling with your feet out, you may feel as if you are sitting up much straighter. This is your correct body position and any additional layback is simply wasted motion. Because the additional movement propels your back beyond its useful arc and then downward, it pushes your weight into the bow of the boat, sinking it beyond its designed waterline. The net result: you waste energy, slow the boat down, and get frustrated.

Recall our earlier discussion of the sculling motion: the legs begin the drive, followed by the back, with the arms finishing the stroke. The idea of rowing connected is not contrary to this since each major muscle group does indeed start pulling in this sequence. The distinction is that these major muscle groups do overlap in the exertion of force, and they all finish together. This allows you to take advantage of each muscle group's ability to add momentum to the drive without losing the momentum generated by the others.

When you have this sequence down correctly, you'll be one of the scullers the uninitiated look at and say, "Geez, that looks so easy I bet I could do it." They'll never know.

Rowing Quiet

Rowing quiet is the art of eliminating each minute technical flaw until you can row at absolute full pressure while appearing to be paddling along. You make it look easy. Sculling quietly also has a literal meaning: When you do it right, your catch and release will be barely audible.

The catch and release are the parts of the stroke to which you want to devote the most attention. Mastering the art of rowing connected will get you part of the way there since your finish will be cleaned up. Remember, one correct movement leads to another correct movement.

The Release

Make sure you are releasing the water with the blades square. If you are not, you may be flipping water up at the release or "throwing a lip," so called because the water trailing off the curved blade takes the form of a lip. Throwing a lip is a sure sign you are probably starting to feather the blades before they are out of the water. To correct this flaw before it becomes a real problem, think of the pressure of the oar handles on the second joint of each finger on the pull-through transferring to the first joint (closest to the palm) as you push down with the fingers and away with the thumbs. Minimize the downward push; think of it as a one inch "tap" down with the hands rather than the hands and shoulders dropping down at the release.

This down-and-away motion within the hands will result in the oar handles resting in the fingers as you begin to move the arms away from the body at the release. This is the "micro" down-and-away; the "macro" down-and-away is the hands themselves dropping down and pushing away from the body. Make sure you understand the distinction. Too many scullers try to finish by simply dropping the wrists down at the finish without moving the oar handles out into the fingers. Although this may work, it reduces the clearance between your hands and thighs

Try this with your eyes closed. Hold the position and feel the connection from your hands through to your feet.

Throwing a lip — exactly what you don't want. The oar should slip quietly out of the water, even at full pressure.

as you continue the recovery motion. When you hit rough water you may find you need that extra clearance. If you do tend to use the wrists to feather and roll up, you may find you develop tendonitis as well. So, either scull fast and painlessly or scull slowly in pain.

The Catch

The other critical part of the stroke is the catch. While the release is important because you want to get the blades out of the water without sacrificing any of the work you did (and speed you generated) on the drive, at the catch you want to ensure you don't slow the boat down when you reverse direction.

If you must be quiet at the release, you must be absolutely silent at the catch. Think about the physics of the catch for a moment. You are propelling your body weight in a direction opposite to the direction you want to go. When you are in the catch position, all your weight is on your feet, you are leaning forward and your arms are fully extended. At this point, in the least stable position possible, you must time your catch to insert the blades into the water at the same speed as the boat. Then you must reverse your direction instantly, without slowing the boat. To further complicate matters, as you reverse direction, you must be sure your blades are anchored in the water and are connected through your body to the footstretchers.

The best way to appreciate the importance of the catch is to have someone videotape you from the dock as you scull. Start from the release position at a dead stop, recover, and take the catch. The first few times you try this, do it with the blades flat at the catch. This is a little more stable than with the blades squared. When you get your confidence up a little, try it with the blades squared and, after you are comfortable with that, an air catch (don't drop the blades into the water at the catch).

When you look at the video, watch the stern just at the catch. If it moves backward before it starts to move forward, you are checking the boat. Multiply the few inches of backward motion by the 250 strokes in a 2000-meter race, and you have dug yourself a sizable hole. Think of stern check as a little present to your competitors. Each inch of stern check per stroke is a little less than a boat length over 2000 meters, or two-and-a-half lengths over a 3-mile head race. Don't be so generous.

All you do at the catch is raise your arms slightly. The blades are squared up, your body is fully compressed, and your arms are extended. You don't need to actually lift your arms. All you need do is unweight the oar handles and the weight of the blades will drop them into the water at the proper depth. The blades don't have to be covered at the catch because as soon as you start pulling, the blade builds a wall of water.

Get the feeling of the proper depth by sitting at the release with straight arms. Raise and lower your hands, first consciously lifting the hands and then simply unweighting the hands, allowing the blades to fall into the water. The blades are at the right depth when they are squared up floating in the water. When you are comfortable in this position, practice this by catching at half slide, concentrating on moving only the arms at the catch. Make sure you aren't lifting with the hands at the catch. Remember, you are allowing the catch to happen, you are not forcing it to happen.

If your hands are small you may find that shaving down the handles gives you more control of the oar around the turn at the release. The handle should fit easily in your fingers.

Concentrate on maintaining the same body position during the last part of the recovery and the first part of the drive. The legs move up, the blades drop in, but the back position and arm position don't change.

Once you have a good idea of the correct feeling, scull at very light pressure at a low rating (16 strokes per minute), again concentrating on moving nothing at the catch but the arms. You may want to row long distances at half pressure, attempting to make the catch as quiet as possible and more relaxed and gentler with each stroke. With practice you will be able to scull with a deft catch at race pace at full power.

A perfect catch is part motion and part timing. The proper time to put the oars in the water is just as you reach full compression, before your start to pull. Think of the catch as the last thing you do on the recovery, not the first part of the drive. Use the presence (or absence) of backsplash as a visible indicator of your catch timing. Some scullers don't believe backsplash is a good thing because it represents a backward force on the boat, but, at least initially, it is essential to ensure your catch is effective.

If at all possible, get videotaped every so often as you work on your catch to monitor your progress. You will see the stern movement steadily decrease as you improve. You can also monitor your stern check when you are sculling. Simply watch your stern just as you take the catch. It should be perfectly still throughout the catch cycle, from before you put the blades in the water to after the drive has been started. The stern should not wiggle from side to side or bounce up or down. You can also watch the V-shaped wake which forms off your stern. Keep the wake steady and flowing. Other ways to monitor stern check include tying a rope around the hull, taping a stick to the sternpost, or both.

For the rope-around-the-hull monitor, you tie a shoestring or other thin-gauge rope to the sternstay of your port rigger, pass it under the hull and tie it to the sternstay of your starboard rigger. I wouldn't try doing this on the water. The purpose served by the rope is simple. It generates a larger and more visible wake. If the wake is continuous and does not disappear or drastically diminish at the catch, you are not checking the boat, or at least not checking it very much. If the wake disappears at the catch, you are stern-checking the boat.

The simplest check monitor is the stick taped to the sternpost. The stick simply provides a sharper visual contrast against the water than the sternpost itself.

Find a straight stick, white or some other easily visible color (a drinking straw works well), and tape it to the stern parallel to the water, projecting about 5 inches out over the water. As you scull, watch the end of the straw move over the water. If it moves smoothly and at a constant speed toward you on the recovery and then instantly reverses direction as you take the catch, you are sculling well. If the stick moves unevenly or seems to hesitate, you need to smooth out your stroke.

Body Control

If you still have stern check after you have a deft catch, you need to work on your body motion. A perfect catch is a combination of bladework and body control; just as the body reaches full compression, the hands unweight the oars and the blades enter the water. Instantly the body reverses direction and the drive begins. Stern check is caused by a lack of coordination between bladework and body movement. If the oars are placed in the water before the body is prepared for the catch or you begin the drive before the oars are buried, you slow down the boat.

Body motion, in turn, has two components. One is position and the other is the sequence of movements. The correct body position for the catch is a function of the recovery. From the release, the arms come out, followed by the back and finally, the legs. Before you are halfway up the slide, all upper body motion should be completed. The arms are straight, shoulders forward, back leaning forward from the hips. The entire body should be relaxed but not limp. There are only two actions left on the recovery: the completion of the recovery on the slide and the roll-up and catch. This lack of motion past the half-slide position is crucial because the closer you get to the stern, the less stable the boat is.

When the back comes out of bow during the first part of the recovery, it should be fairly straight. A lot of scullers, even fast ones, hunch over; instead, sit up by decreasing the angle between your legs and back. On the drive, the upright posture helps you hang your weight on the oars by providing a better connection between the arms and legs. It also expands the chest, giving your lungs and diaphragm more room to expand, increasing the amount of oxygen you can inhale. The back should not lean to one side for any reason. If you are trying to balance the boat by leaning you run the risk of hurting yourself as you pull from an unstable position. It is also much easier and more efficient to use handle height, rather than side-to-side body lean, to control balance.

The turnaround, the part of the stroke when the slide reverses direction at the catch, is critical. At the instant the blades enter the water, begin the leg drive. Again, the rest of the body is absolutely quiet. The back connects the legs to the oar handles, and the sensation is one of the feet pressing down into the stretchers and the oar handles pressing firmly into the second, or middle joint, of the fingers. The turnaround should be a very fast, immediate reversal with no hesitation or "feeling" for the water. If your bladework is correct, the oars will be where they are supposed to be. Make sure the back is stable; don't try to increase the feel of driving at the catch by starting the back too early or by lunging out at the catch for a little extra reach. Also, remember that the quickness of the reversal in direction does not mean your leg drive should be a quick kick. Unless you incorporate King Kong's strength in Don Knotts' physique, a quick kick will not overcome the inertia of the boat in the instant you lock your blades into the water.

Some scullers drive off the balls of their feet; I have found it more effective to drive off the whole foot throughout the drive. Ted Nash of Penn A.C. refers to pushing off the ball of the foot as "cushioning" the leg drive, certainly something to avoid. Whether you drive off the ball of your foot or the whole foot is usually a function of the flexibility of your Achilles tendon and the position of the shoes. The lower the heels of the shoes, the easier it will be to drive off the entire foot. One thing you may want to consider is that if you drive off the ball of the foot, the calf (specifically the gastrocnemius and associated muscles) is the lone initial connecting muscle on the drive. If and when these muscles tire, the connection deteriorates. A drive off the whole foot eliminates this potential problem.

Adapting to Conditions

There will be times when you will need to modify your technique somewhat due to conditions. In reality, you are not modifying your stroke, you are simply emphasizing one part more than another. For example, when sculling into a headwind, you should concentrate on getting the hands out quickly to keep the rating up and maintaining your length by emphasizing good layback into the bow. You may also want to delay your roll-up until just before the catch to minimize the effect of the wind on your blades.

In a tailwind, you should emphasize pulling the boat up underneath you using the toes. This will help prevent rushing the slide.

A crosswind is perhaps the most difficult type of wind to scull through. Unless you are in very sheltered waters, the crosswind's effects will be magnified by the waves hitting you from the side. This combination requires excellent control of hand levels, especially at the catch. Don't be tentative in a stiff crosswind. Make sure you come up and catch assertively. Any hang or other delay at the catch will have

There is very little stern check here. Note that the wake remains close to the hull, even just before the catch.

The sculler is driving sideways (look at his knees), so the boat is moving in the same direction. Not the fastest way to the finish line.

terrible effects on your balance. Emphasize the pressure on the handles and stretchers all the way into the body. By maintaining pressure through the strong finish you will support each side of the boat and maintain stability. Finally, don't lean or shift your legs to one side to balance.

Drills

Feet-out Sculling.

Purpose: To emphasize connecting the body all the way through the drive. This drill was also incorporated in the basic technique chapter as a release drill.

Description: Scull at various pressures with the feet resting on top of the shoes. Row complete, long strokes with the same layback used when sculling normally. Emphasize feeling the pressure on the feet and the insides of the fingers all the way through the drive, especially at the finish.

Process: This drill is as simple to execute as it sounds. The tough part is building the confidence to finish the stroke without hunching over the handles at the release.

Start sculling at a low rating, trying to keep the feet pressed down on the stretchers throughout the drive. During the drive, as the back starts to come on, make sure the shoulders are also pulling back. Once the shoulders and back have completed their part of the drive, concentrate on holding them in that position as the arms come in. Feel the pressure of the oar handles on the inside of the fingers as the arms finish the stroke. Think of that pressure on the fingers as a vector of force, connecting up through the arms, down the back and hips, down the legs and into the footstretchers until the release.

When you are somewhat comfortable sculling with your feet out, try increasing the pressure. You don't need to do this at full pressure, but a solid half to three-quarters pressure will help you get the feeling of hanging on the oars all the way through the drive. Keep the drive, particularly the leg drive, steady and continuous. If you tend to kick off quickly at the catch, it will show up here because your feet will rise three to six inches out of the stretchers at the release. In extreme cases you may find you drive yourself off the seat and into the water; so don't start this drill in February if you scull in a northern latitude.

Incorporate this drill into your daily workout early in the season. The best time is just after you shove off from the dock. Scull with the arms only, feeling the feet press into the shoes, then with the arms and back, and finally row full slide. Slowly increase the pressure and scull that way for several minutes. After you have stopped to tie in, concentrate on transmitting the feeling you had when sculling feet out to your normal sculling.

You may find it helpful to go back to this drill every so often during the season to ensure you are sculling connected.

Straight-arm Sculling.

Purpose: To develop a quicker catch and eliminate problems caused by not fully extending the arms at the catch. "Quicker" catches normally mean earlier catches, i.e. unweighting the hands earlier on the recovery. This drill is also useful for emphasizing the legs and the back as the main power sources for the early part of the drive.

If you want to focus just on the beginning of the drive and the use of the legs, shorten your stroke to the first six inches of the slide. Be careful to keep the speed into and away from the catch equal and steady. If you are moving away from the catch too quickly, you are probably not connected and might well be shooting your tail.

Description: Scull continuously at any pressure at a fairly low rating; below 25 is fine. From the finish, extend the arms, continue the recovery, take the catch, and begin the drive as you normally would. However, do not bend the arms; instead, finish the stroke when the legs are down and the back is in bow. At the finish the arms are straight as the hands push the oars down and away. Watch the stern and the wake off the stern to note any stern check.

Again, feel the connection between the handles and the footstretcher throughout this abbreviated drive. Keep the handles level throughout the drive; do not start to pull them down into the lap as the arms near the finish.

Scull this way for a few minutes, then add the arms and feel the difference. Switch between the drill and normal sculling, focusing on feeling the legs, back, and arms working in sequence, one phasing in as the other is phasing out. As with any drill, the first few strokes of normal sculling are very important; concentrate on the "feel" of the stroke at that time.

Process: This drill can be incorporated in workouts two or three times a week early in the season. Use this drill occasionally to help correct technical problems such as a bent arm at the catch.

Slide, Catch, and Row.

Purpose: To improve recovery timing, entry of blades into the water, and connection of the drive.

Description: In calm water, sit at the finish with your eyes fixed on the stern. While maintaining a steady gaze on the stern (or stick attached to the stern), tap the hands down one inch to release the water, feather, move the arms away from the body, and continue the recovery by pivoting forward from the hips. Complete the recovery by rolling the blades up, catch, drive, and pause with the hands at the body after the release. Let the boat glide, then check the boat until it is stopped, and repeat.

Process: Watch the stern throughout the drill, looking to see if a V-shaped wake appears immediately after the catch and beginning of the drive. If not, there is some slippage or slack in the power connection. Look also to see if the stern is slipping backwards at the catch; if so timing is off and the sculler is stern-checking the boat.

If you have a slipping problem or are otherwise checking the boat, there are several things you can do to address the problem. You may need to get your hands out before you swing the back over from the hips; get your body angle over before your legs break and the seat moves towards the stern; square the blades up earlier; relax more throughout this sequence; unweight the handles earlier, or perhaps some or all of the above.

This drill is quite simple and can be done at any time during the season and at any time during your row. You may find it especially useful in helping to maintain

Straight-arm sculling feels weird at first, but stick with it — it's a big help if you break your arms too soon on the drive.

Slide, catch, and row: You also can start the drill from the hands-away position when you want to focus on the pivot and slide. Also, it helps to keep the hands moving around the turn.

concentration if you are doing pieces with friends and have to wait for them to catch up after each piece.

No-Pressure Catch, Quarter-Pressure Finish.

Purpose: To improve the drive connection at the finish and emphasize the feeling of accelerating through the drive. This drill teaches the overlapping and connected nature of the drive. It gets you into the habit of increasing the pressure through the drive and accelerating the boat itself so that at the release the boat is moving at its greatest speed. It will also show how easy the release becomes if you are able to connect the drive all the way through to the finish.

Description: Scull continuously but apply no pressure at the catch; build the pressure all the way through the stroke to a quarter (or more) pressure at the release. Try to row this drill with blades squared.

A variation on this drill is called the "swing and pick." Many scullers begin each row with this drill. It is quite simple, and is performed by breaking the stroke down into its component parts. Start out from the finish and scull smoothly using only the arms, keeping the back and legs immobile. Keep the cadence very low and concentrate on drawing smoothly and firmly all the way into the release. After 20 strokes or so, add the back for 20, then half slide, then full slide. Each time additional body parts come into play, re-emphasize the acceleration into the finish.

Some scullers perform the swing-and-pick drill at high cadence and seem to slap at the water. This serves no useful purpose and actually encourages poor sculling. The point of the drill is not to row at an impossibly high cadence, it is to emphasize the connection of the body by accelerating into the release.

Process: Scull continuously at no pressure, quarter pressure for long stretches of a mile or more. Maintain concentration throughout the piece and maintain the increasing pressure as well. This drill is useful throughout the year, and the swing-and-pick drill version is a good way to scull away from the dock as it reinforces the basic motion, sequence, and connectedness of the sculling stroke.

If you do use the swing-and-pick drill as part of your warm-up, do not let your mind wander. Familiarity breeds contempt, and this is especially true in the warm-up. The mind often has not made the transition from the bed, the desk, or the job to the boat; errant thoughts interfere with sculling. If you find you have this mental focus deficiency problem, make sure you are correctly using your pre-row time by visualizing the upcoming workout.

Windmilling.

Purpose: To provide a better feel for the unweighting of the hands at the catch.

Description: Scull at a low rate, quarter to half pressure or just enough to keep the boat moving steadily. After the release, as the hands and arms move away from the body and extend, consciously push down on the handles by increasing the weight of the hands on the oar handles. Do this slowly and in a relaxed, almost gentle way. With your peripheral vision, watch the blades head up into the sky. After the legs begin to break, slowly decrease the weight on the oar handles by allowing the weight of the blades to lift the hands up. Feel the handles rise toward the catch. Continue rolling forward on the slide and rolling the blades up to the squared position. At the end of the recovery, the hands are completely unweighted and the blades complete their controlled fall into the water. Drive and repeat.

Process: Alternate ten strokes or so of this sculling with ten normal strokes. Feel the differences, but more importantly feel the similarities between the two.

This is a drill for more advanced scullers because the windmill position, with the blades far off the water, is inherently unstable and encourages flipping.

Chapter Six
Exercise Physiology

ne of the biggest causes of frustration among scullers is their lack of a basic understanding of exercise physiology. Too many good, dedicated, competent athletes never achieve half of what they are capable of because they don't train intelligently.

One of my goals with this book is to make all the techno-speak of the exercise physiologist mean something to the sculler who has little background beyond high school biology.

Today's racing times are a lot faster than times recorded thirty years ago: Eights are about 35 seconds faster over 2000 meters. The winning time at the 1960 Olympics was a 5:57 by Karl Adam's legendary Ratzeburg crew. That is not good enough to get them into the semifinals these days and probably not even enough to win a fast college race. The same 1960 Olympics saw the Russian sculler Ivanov win the singles in 7:14; Thomas Lange had to row a 6:49 to win the gold in the 1988 Olympics.

Some of this additional speed is undoubtedly due to a bigger pool of athletes, more efficient hull design, and lighter oars. Better technique may also play a role, but most of the improvement is due to a better understanding and application of the principles of exercise physiology.

Scullers come in all shapes and sizes, from Pertti Karpinnen at 220 pounds and well over 6 feet to Ruggero Verocca at 5'6" and 158 pounds to Rebecca Sage at 5'8" and 127 pounds. Some of the most impressive physical specimens are the slowest and some of the most unimposing people are the fastest. If there is an ideal somatotype (body type) for a sculler, it is an ectomesomorph (also known as a tall, lanky, muscular individual). If your parents provided you with this frame, you have good leverage and little excess fat to haul down the course. Since sculling is simply applying power to a system of levers to move a mass, the type of levers and amount and distribution of mass are important considerations. If you do not precisely fit this ideal prototype, you'll just have to compensate by taking advantage of your other strengths.

Many scullers overtrain or concentrate on one aspect of their sculling almost exclusively. If you want to go as fast as you are physically and mentally able, you'll have to understand your unique physiological characteristics and what sculling demands of them. It is important for you to understand how your body produces energy, how muscle cell activity affects the body's main systems, and the implications those processes hold for your sculling.

MUSCLE CELL PHYSIOLOGY

The average person has some 65 billion cells, all highly specialized and totally interdependent. Of these, 25 to 50 percent are muscle cells. Groups of muscle cells are connected to the brain by nerves that sense both position and level of pain, and control speed, angle, and force of contraction in the muscle. These groups are called motor units. In turn, a muscle, such as the bicep, is comprised of many motor units. Muscle cells and their attached nerves actually are a single fully integrated unit.

The cell gets the energy it needs to do the bidding of the motor nerve from two sources within the cell. The mitochondria produce energy aerobically (with oxygen), so the more mitochondria you have and the more efficient they are, the more aerobic energy you'll be able to produce. Other components of the muscle cell are used in producing energy anaerobically (without oxygen).

Muscle-fiber Typing

Muscle cells are "typed" by the motor nerves that control them. A cell is either fast twitch (FT) or slow twitch (ST) because the motor nerve controlling it is either a fast-twitch or slow-twitch nerve.

The structural and chemical differences between fast-twitch and slow-twitch cells enable the fast-twitch cell to contract three times faster and generate power very quickly. This speed and power-production capacity makes FT cells ten times stronger than ST cells. Sprinters and weight lifters usually have high percentages of fast-twitch fibers to produce a lot of energy very quickly.

As one might expect, slow-twitch cells do not generate as much power and are slower to contract. Compared with fast-twitch fibers, slow-twitch fibers have a relatively large aerobic capacity but a limited anaerobic capacity. In athletes with high percentages of ST fibers, this large aerobic capacity leads to higher oxygen uptake levels, lower lactic acid output, and the ability to engage in long exercise bouts before exhaustion sets in.

Slow-twitch fibers are so effective at aerobic energy production because the individual cells contain large quantities of the chemical compounds and fuel sources needed to produce ATP (the compound that provides energy for muscular contraction) via the aerobic energy system.

The ST cell has several other characteristics that differ from FT cells in general. ST cells are surrounded by capillaries, which supply the cell with oxygen and substrates—substances that can be transformed to energy—and remove carbon dioxide and water, by-products of the aerobic energy process. The presence of the capillaries means any waste products are quickly removed from the cell. The stores of the substances and the enzymes necessary to produce much energy anaerobically are limited in ST cells.

There is a subset of FT cells that shares many characteristics with ST cells. Fast-twitch oxidative, or FTO cells, fall roughly between ST and FT cells in their energy sources, fatigability, and therefore speed of contraction. Oxidative refers to this cell's ability to use the aerobic energy system as an energy source. This ability, coupled with the high power output of the FT cell, enables FTO cells to put out a lot of power without producing the large amounts of lactic acid one would normally expect.

	Slow twitch	Fast twitch	FTO
Speed of contraction	Slow	Fast	Medium
Primary energy source	Aerobic	Lactic acid	Aerobic, lactic acid
Power output ability	Low	High	Medium
Endurance	High	Low	Medium
Vascularization	High	Low	High
Oxygen storage capacity	High	Low	Medium
Waste products	CO_2, H_2O	CO_2, lactic acid	CO_2, H_2O, lactic acid
Oxidative enzyme content	High	Low	High

There is solid evidence that within certain limits you can alter the percentage of the various types of cells within your muscles. Individuals may acquire FTO cells as a result of a long, steady-state training program. The increased aerobic capacity of the FTO cell may simply be the result of a "regular" FT cell adapting to the type of energy production required by the training regimen.

Your muscle-fiber type will have a big influence on your training and racing strategy, but the "wrong" type of fiber will not reduce your competitive ability unless you are trying for the Olympics.

MUSCLES AND NERVES

There are two types of nerves: efferent—or sensory—nerves, and afferent—or motor—nerves, which control muscular action. Afferent nerves transmit information from the motor cortex of the brain to the muscle. Each muscle is controlled by a specific part of the motor cortex, which communicates with its assigned muscle by sending electrical impulses via motor nerves. Motor nerves, together with one to several hundred muscle cells they control, make up motor units.

When the nerve impulse reaches the junction where the nerve connects to the muscle (the neuromuscular junction) the motor nerve triggers a muscle cell contraction by releasing a minute amount of a chemical compound. This is followed almost immediately by the release of another compound that tells your muscle fibers to stop contracting.

The large muscles, such as the vastus lateralis (the big muscle on the outside of the upper leg) have many muscle cells per motor nerve because they do not perform fine, precise movements. Conversely, muscle cells controlling extremely precise movements, such as focusing the eye, may each have their own motor nerve.

One of our most interesting and complicated abilities is that of matching strength to the task. A motor unit either contracts completely or not at all, so when a nerve impulse is sent to a motor unit, the motor unit cannot vary the strength of

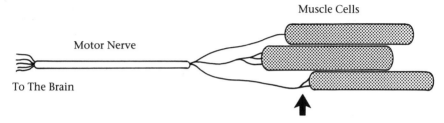

The muscle-nerve system.

Muscle Cells

Motor Nerve

To The Brain

Release of the chemicals controlling
muscle cell contraction occurs
at the neuromuscular junction

the contraction. However, each muscle is comprised of many motor units, which are recruited by the brain in a fixed, preset sequence so you use only the exact number of muscle cells you need to accomplish the task at hand.

The other means of controlling the amount of force exerted by a muscle is by the frequency of contraction of the individual motor units. If an impulse is sent to a motor unit to contract, and another impulse is sent before the motor relaxes, the motor unit contracts with more force. The process is known as summation; the effects of the additional impulses cause the force of contraction to increase, or summate.

Efferent nerves sense heat, cold, position, pressure, and other sensations that give the brain the information it needs to determine what action to take. Sensory nerves provide you with all the information you need to scull: They tell you the position of your arms, the amount of pressure on the insides of the fingers, the pain level in the quadriceps, the position of your competition, and the thousand other bits of information you process every moment.

The two parts of the sensory system, the inner ear and position receptors, work together so your body knows what it is doing. The inner ear acts as a gyroscope, giving you a sense of balance. The position receptors in the joints, tendons, and muscles work together with the inner ear to provide you with a sense of spatial positioning. This sense allows you, without looking, to know where each part of your body is in relation to every other part.

Receptors are differentiated by their location in the body. For example, joint receptors trigger when a joint reaches the end of its range of motion; a tendon receptor increases its firing as its muscle's tension increases, and the muscle receptor assesses the length of the muscle and how quickly it contracts. The entire system enables you to keep track of yourself as you scull.

ORGAN SYSTEMS

Physiologists have organized the body into 11 functional systems, all interdependent, yet each playing a distinct role in maintaining and supporting human life.

The most important systems to scullers are the muscular, respiratory, and cardiovascular. Here is a sculling-specific review of these functional systems.

Cardiovascular System

The cardiovascular system is comprised of the blood, the heart, and the vessels carrying blood throughout the body. To go back to freshman biology for a moment, remember that the arteries carry blood to the muscles, capillaries deliver blood to individual cells, and veins return the "used" blood to the heart and lungs.

Blood is a very complex liquid that performs a number of vital functions. It carries oxygen, enzymes, and nutrients from the digestive system to the muscle cells, carries carbon dioxide and other wastes away from the muscles, and delivers infection-fighting agents to damaged areas. Blood also works to maintain normal body pH and temperature, regulates the water content of cells, and transports hormones from the endocrine system. Although there are many different types of cells that comprise the blood, scullers are most concerned with the red blood cell.

The red blood cell is responsible for transporting oxygen and carbon dioxide, and can do little else. Because it is so specialized, it cannot repair itself; the average life of the red blood cell is 120 days. Because the average female has about 4.8 million red blood cells per cubic millimeter of blood and the average male 5.4 million, the body has to work constantly to replace lost red blood cells. In fact, you produce about 2 million red blood cells every second. Probably didn't know you worked so hard all the time.

Although the red blood cell has a very limited role, it is a crucial one. The red blood cell picks up oxygen in the lungs by binding oxygen to the hemoglobin contained in the red blood cell. When the cell gets to a muscle or other cell that needs the oxygen, it releases that oxygen and picks up carbon dioxide. The carbon dioxide is then transported back to the lungs where it is released.

Endurance athletes tend to have a higher concentration of red blood cells than non-athletes because the body adapts to the stress of training by increasing the number of red blood cells. This adaptation is triggered by certain cells in the kidney. When these cells become oxygen-deficient, they release a hormone that triggers increased red blood cell production.

People who do not have sufficient oxygen-carrying capacity are sometimes referred to as anemic. Anemia means that either the number of red blood cells, or the hemoglobin content of those cells, is low. Although anemia can be caused by many things, the lack of iron or vitamin B-12 are two of the more common explanations. A deficiency in either one can be due to inadequate diet or disease. In either case, anemia can be a significant problem for the sculler because it can drastically reduce your ability to get oxygen to your muscles and rid them of carbon dioxide. If you are tired all the time, pale, and get cold easily, anemia may be your problem. Do not self-diagnose your situation, get to a doctor and have her, or him, figure out your problem.

If there is a "most important organ" besides the brain, it is the heart. At its most basic level, the heart is simply a pump. Physically, the heart can be described as a hollow, muscular organ situated behind the sternum and between the lungs that in untrained folks is about the size of their fist. For you longtime scullers, the heart can be significantly larger due to the stresses placed on it during training.

The heart is divided into four chambers, each of which has a specific role. The two smaller chambers on the top of the heart are the atria, the two larger ones below are the ventricles. The heart is really two separate and distinct pumps, with each atrium paired with the ventricle underlying it. The atrium is connected to its corresponding ventricle by valves. The right side of the heart pumps the blood through the lungs and the left side of the heart pumps the reoxygenated blood back into the body.

The strongest one of the chambers is also the one most affected by training, the left ventricle. This strength is illustrated by the left ventricle's thick, muscular walls, which are needed to push the blood through the thousands of miles of vessels throughout your body. Training has two effects on the left ventricle. Endurance training enlarges the chamber because your muscles are using oxygen and producing carbon dioxide at a rapid rate. The ventricle adapts to meet this stress of training by increasing the amount of blood it can pump during each beat.

The well-trained (and genetically fortunate) sculler has a heart that can pump six times more blood than the heart of the average, untrained sofa spud.

The heart also adapts to the stress placed on it by power athletes such as weight lifters and the like. These people are constantly forcing their muscles to contract vigorously, restricting the blood vessels within the muscles. The more restricted the blood vessels, the more difficult it is to pump blood through them. The power athlete's heart adapts by becoming stronger. This adaptation can be seen in the increased thickness of the wall of the left ventricle.

In the early days of sports some physicians thought the enlargement of the heart was a pathological sign; it indicated illness or disease. This theory arose when physicians determined that some hypertensive people had enlarged left ventricles because the hypertension made it hard for the heart to pump blood. Thus, the heart adapted to the "conditioning stresses" of hypertension. Since doctors saw that people with enlarged left ventricles had serious health problems, some of them figured that all people with enlarged left ventricles were candidates for an early death. When these scientists saw an enlarged left ventricle in an athlete, they diagnosed it as an "athlete's heart" and recommended complete rest and the cessation of all activity. Just when the guy was getting fast, too.

Cardiac output is determined by two things, your pulse rate and the amount of blood pumped each minute by your trusty left ventricle. In turn, your pulse rate is determined by your body's demand for oxygen. The greater the demand, the higher the pulse rate. Individuals' maximal heart rates vary considerably depending on genetic makeup. Generally speaking, endurance athletes have a lower maximal heart rate than normal humans. This tendency is due to the larger size of the athlete's heart, which makes it more difficult to contract at a rapid rate.

The amount of blood pumped by the heart during each beat, or the stroke volume, is determined by the amount of blood returning to the heart. When you're exercising vigorously, your muscles need large quantities of oxygen and they produce a lot of carbon dioxide. This requires lots of blood, which is returned in large quantities to the heart, filling it and stretching the left ventricle. Muscle contracts more forcefully when it is prestretched. Since the left ventricle has the same habits as your other muscles, the more it is stretched the more forcefully it contracts. The demand of the muscles and other organs determines how much blood your heart pumps and how vigorously it pumps it.

Respiratory System

The respiratory system is comprised of the lungs and associated breathing passages, the vocal cords, the larynx, and a host of other parts.

The lungs resemble a pair of large, cone-shaped sponges. They perform two main functions: replenishing oxygen in the blood and removing carbon dioxide from the blood.

When you breathe in, oxygen permeates the lungs. Since the blood in the area around the lungs is "used," it has little oxygen in it. The air you breathe contains quite a bit more oxygen, allowing the blood to absorb oxygen until it is saturated. Carbon dioxide exchange is just the reverse. Carbon dioxide, a waste product generated by muscle cells, is transferred from the "used" blood, where it is relatively highly concentrated, back to the lungs, where it is present in relatively low concentrations. From there, it is exhaled.

These transfer processes take place in the alveoli, small, spongy sacs distributed throughout the lungs. The larger your lungs, the faster you breathe, or both, the more oxygen you can use and the more carbon dioxide you can get rid of. There seems to be little you can do to increase the size of your lungs, so to take in more oxygen or blow off more carbon dioxide, breathe faster. Altering your breathing rate will not have any positive effect on your performance and may well slow you down.

In the old days scullers, cyclists, and other endurance athletes tried to develop an ability to control their breathing. They thought that by controlling their respiration they could improve their performance. Recent studies show the opposite effect can be expected. Your body naturally sets the optimal respiratory rate given the level of exertion you have selected. So don't try to control your breathing; this is one of those rare things you don't have to concern yourself with in your quest to be the ultimate sculler.

Muscular System

Muscles provide motion, maintain posture, and produce heat. There are three types of muscles: cardiac, or heart muscle; visceral muscle, the muscle that creates internal motion such as contraction of the stomach to churn food; and skeletal muscle, the muscle of interest to scullers.

A muscle is not simply a group of muscle cells. It consists of the covering over the muscle itself, the connective tissue joining it to other muscle or to bone, and the muscle's nerve and blood supply.

The covering over the muscle, known as the fascia, serves a number of purposes: holding the muscles together, carrying nerves and blood vessels, and in some cases storing fat and water. The fascia is often continuous with the connective tissue that attaches the muscle to another body structure, such as a muscle or bone. One of the more common connective tissues is the tendon.

The blood flow for a particular muscle is usually handled by an artery and a vein or two. The blood vessels commonly follow the path of the motor nerve powering that muscle, with capillaries branching off periodically to ensure each muscle cell is in contact with at least one capillary.

A Final Thought

The next time you work out devote some of your mental effort to thinking about the various processes going on in your body as you train. Learn to listen to your body with the same intensity and understanding the classical conductor feels for the orchestra. By combining the science of the physiologist with your actual experience and knowledge, you will become a more intelligent and therefore, more successful athlete.

Chapter Seven

Energy Sources

fter technique, perhaps the most important factor in determining potential speed is the ability of the sculler to produce and use energy. Another key determining factor is the body's ability to deal with by-products of the energy processes. Understanding the principles behind the energy systems will help you build the training program that will best suit you. It will also help you modify your training program as your physiology, skill level, and aspirations change.

ATP

Muscle cells produce movement by contracting. The only energy source enabling the muscle to contract is a chemical compound called adenosine triphosphate, or ATP. Because ATP is the immediate energy source for all human activity, it deserves your close attention.

Most of your physical conditioning has been or will be designed to enhance your body's ability to produce, use, store, transport, and resynthesize ATP. ATP is strange stuff. It never really goes away, rather it is broken down to produce energy and then resynthesized back into ATP in a continuous cycle. The resynthesis of ATP requires fuel, which is indirectly supplied by the breakdown of different types of food.

Food that can be broken down into a form usable by one of the energy systems is called a substrate. These substrates, such as glucose (sugar carried in the blood), produce ATP indirectly by supplying the fuel needed to re-form ATP. Substrates are not transformed into ATP, they simply provide the fuel necessary to rebuild ATP.

ATP-PI RESYNTHESIS CYCLE

ATP is broken down by the splitting of the chemical bonds within the compound, liberating energy (which is used to contract the muscle), and leaving the remnants of the compound. These remnants are known as ADP (adenosine diphosphate) and Pi (inorganic phosphate), as shown in the illustration of the ATP resysnthesis cycle.

To get a better grasp on this, think of a hydroelectric dam. The water flowing through the dam provides energy to drive the turbines that produce electricity. The water is analogous to the food substrate in that it doesn't perform the work, it drives the process that produces usable energy. The usable energy is analogous to ATP.

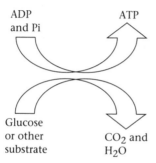

The ATP resynthesis cycle.

ADP and Pi → ATP

Glucose or other substrate → CO_2 and H_2O

The three methods your body uses to resynthesize ATP all operate in the same basic manner. The fuel stored in the food you eat is released through these energy systems, forcing the ADP and Pi compounds back together, reforming ATP. The differences between the three energy systems lie in the source of the fuel driving the process, the amount of ATP produced, and the by-products of the process.

ATP is quantified by the mole—a given amount of a chemical compound by weight; a mole of glucose weighs 180 grams. One mole of ATP produces between 7 and 12 kilocalories (kcal) of energy when broken down completely. The kilocalorie is a unit of work or energy; the average male consumes about 2,300 kcal of energy in daily life without any exercise. At rest, your body produces a mole of ATP every 10 to 15 minutes. During maximal exercise you may produce a mole of ATP every minute, and those of you who train hard and smart can do significantly better. Keep this fun fact in mind as you learn more about the energy systems used in sculling.

ANAEROBIC ENERGY SYSTEMS

Two of the energy systems produce energy anaerobically, or without oxygen.

Phosphagen System

The most basic anaerobic system is the phosphagen system. Since the amount of energy produced by the phosphagen system is only just enough for a racing start, this is not a terribly important energy system for scullers.

The chemical compound used by the phosphagen system to rebuild ATP within the muscle cell is a very short-term fuel. There is enough of it within the cell to provide ATP for at best ten seconds of maximal effort.

Lactic Acid System

The second anaerobic energy system is known as the lactic acid system, which uses sugar as a fuel source. The sugar is broken down in a process known as anaerobic glycolysis to produce energy. Like the other energy systems, anaerobic glycolysis involves the resynthesis of ATP within the muscle cell.

Glycolysis is simply the breaking down of glycogen (sugar stored in the liver and muscle), so anaerobic glycolysis is the breakdown of glycogen without oxygen. Energy released during this breakdown is used to resynthesize ATP through a complicated series of chemical processes. However, the breakdown of glycogen is not a complete process and one of the by-products is lactic acid.

Anaerobic glycolysis is a very inefficient method of producing energy. It produces less than one-thirteenth of the energy delivered when an equal amount of sugar is broken down with oxygen, or aerobically.

On the plus side, anaerobic glycolysis is a ready source of energy for intense but relatively short bouts of exercise. It is pretty much tapped out after two to three minutes of intense effort, not because you run out of muscle glycogen but because the body cannot tolerate any more accumulation of lactic acid. Lactic acid is thought to produce fatigue in muscles when it accumulates to high enough levels. Thus, the factor limiting the amount of energy you can obtain from anaerobic glycolysis (about 1 to 1.2 moles of usable ATP) is your lactic acid tolerance level.

In test situations, elite scullers have produced so much lactic acid that the resulting blood acid levels would be considered terminal in a hospital patient. If you are able to produce that much lactic acid, you may just wish you were dead.

AEROBIC ENERGY SYSTEM

Scullers' single most important energy system is the aerobic system, which is by far the most efficient means of producing energy. This system delivers thirteen times the amount of ATP produced by the lactic acid system from the same amount of glycogen. And its by-products, carbon dioxide and water, are disposed of quite easily.

The aerobic system produces 75 percent of the energy used in a 2000 meter race and 85 percent to 90 percent of the energy required in a three-mile race. It is comprised of scores of complicated chemical interactions occurring in a precise sequence. These chemical interactions can be grouped into three distinct segments: aerobic glycolysis, the Krebs cycle, and the electron transport system.

During a workout, remember that the phosphagen system can produce only a little more than half a mole of ATP, and the lactic acid system perhaps 1 to 1.2 moles, before you shut down from the effects of acid accumulation.

Aerobic glycolysis, the breaking down of glycogen, produces 3 moles of ATP from each mole of glycogen. This is the same amount produced by anaerobic glycolysis (remember the factor limiting energy production in the lactic acid system is the lactic acid produced, not the ATP produced).

Because oxygen is present during aerobic glycolysis, pyruvic acid—not lactic acid—is produced. Pyruvic acid is then used in the next step in the aerobic system, the Krebs cycle.

No ATP is directly produced during the Krebs cycle; rather the function of the Krebs cycle is to continue the breakdown of glycogen and produce the substrate for the final step in the process.

The last part of the aerobic system, the electron transport system, is a complicated process that produces 36 moles of ATP from the original mole of glycogen. The only by-product of this process is water.

During exercise you don't use one of the energy systems exclusively; at almost all intensities you use at least two of the three systems. For example, during a seven-minute-plus, all-out effort such as one might encounter in a single sculling race, you'll begin by using the phosphagen and lactic acid systems for the first 60 to 90 seconds of the event. The aerobic energy system will need that much time to respond to the increased demand from the muscles. The aerobic system carries you through the majority of the race until the sprint begins and you once again tap into the lactic acid system for the extra energy your muscles require.

The transition between the different energy systems is marked by a gradual takeover of energy production by the aerobic system, which is still assisted by the lactic acid system, even during the body of a race. In the last stage of a race, the lactic acid system's contribution increases somewhat, but only if you have some unused capacity in this system. If you don't have any unused capacity, you better be ahead.

In terms of a percentage of the total effort required in a 2000 meter sculling race, the phosphagen system probably delivers 5 percent of the energy required, the lactic acid system 20 percent and the aerobic system 75 percent. A three-mile race will rely almost totally on the aerobic system. These percentages should be an important consideration in conditioning and training schedules.

ANAEROBIC THRESHOLD

Anaerobic threshold (AT) is the most important physiological concept in the book. While there's some dispute concerning the measurement, theory, and physiological implications of anaerobic threshold, the general consensus seems to be that it is a very important indicator of a sculler's potential athletic performance. The higher your anaerobic threshold, the more energy you can produce before your body starts manufacturing lactic acid in significant quantities. The more energy you can produce without generating lactic acid, the faster you will be, and the less it will hurt. You can exercise until your energy runs out because your performance time will not be limited by the by-products of the energy production processes.

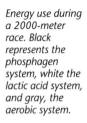

Energy use during a 2000-meter race. Black represents the phosphagen system, white the lactic acid system, and gray, the aerobic system.

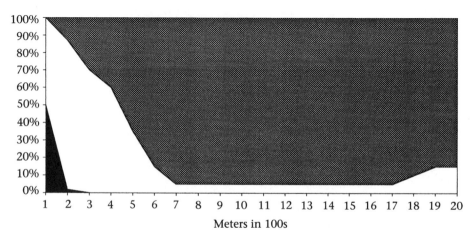

Meters in 100s

Simply stated, the anaerobic threshold is the point at which the energy demands you are placing on your body cannot be entirely met by the aerobic system. At this point, your body starts producing energy anaerobically as well as aerobically.

Once measured, anaerobic threshold can be described in various ways. One of the more precise methods is to quantify AT in terms of the amount of oxygen one can use at the anaerobic threshold. You may see an athlete's AT described as 50ml/kg, which means that the athlete crosses his anaerobic threshold at the point when he is consuming more than 50 milliliters of oxygen per kilogram of body weight. If the athlete's body weight fluctuates significantly, AT as a function of body weight will fluctuate as well. However, the heart rate at which AT is reached will not change due solely to a decrease or increase in weight.

Because heart rate changes during exercise are consistent, heart rate also can be used to evaluate anaerobic threshold, but only as part of a comprehensive exercise test. Increases in heart rate parallel increases in the amount of work performed—up to a point. That point is the anaerobic threshold. At work levels above AT, heart rate increases do not parallel work-load increases; heart rate increases begin to drop. This decrease in the rate of increase makes sense when you consider that the lactic acid system is not using oxygen to produce energy, enabling you to perform more work than you could if you used the aerobic energy system exclusively.

The "Trainability" of AT

Up to a point AT can be altered through intelligent training. The anaerobic threshold you are born with is determined, in large part, by your muscle-fiber type. The higher the percentage of slow-twitch fibers, the higher the anaerobic threshold.

The relationship between fiber type and anaerobic threshold is quite logical. Consider the physiology of the slow-twitch muscle cell. It is specifically designed to produce energy aerobically and has limited quantities of the enzymes and substrates needed for anaerobic metabolism. Compared to a fast-twitch cell the slow-twitch cell cannot produce nearly as much carbon dioxide, lactic acid, or both.

Conversely, the large, strong, fast-twitch cell is designed to operate anaerobically. This specificity of design results in a powerful performance accompanied by lots of heavy breathing due to carbon dioxide and lactic acid production.

Remember the FTO cells from Chapter 6? FTO cells fit in somewhere between pure slow-twitch and pure fast-twitch cells. Because FTO cells appear to be modified FT cells (probably modified as a result of conditioning), they are capable of producing a lot of lactic acid while still operating aerobically. This combination allows the cell to produce energy when the athlete is exercising at intensity levels below AT, increasing the maximal oxygen uptake level. However, this increased maximal ability may or may not be accompanied by a raised anaerobic threshold.

Although AT seems to be originally determined by muscle-fiber type, it appears that AT levels can be raised up to 50 percent through an intelligently applied training program. The average untrained American may have to deal with an anaerobic threshold level of 35 percent (percent of maximal oxygen uptake); a dedicated sculler with a lot of help from his parents and vigorous AT training may be able to attain AT levels of 90 percent.

This "trainability" feature of AT is especially important when you consider the most you can increase your maximal oxygen uptake is around 30 percent. For those with average maximal oxygen uptake levels, the only way to compete with the genetically more fortunate is to increase anaerobic thresholds. Increasing your AT will increase the amount of work you can do without going anaerobic. This is important because the sculler in the next lane over may have a higher maximal oxygen uptake, but because you have a higher anaerobic threshold, you will be able to aerobically row right past him as he struggles with an increasingly painful lactic acid accumulation problem.

There seems to be a strong correlation between scullers with high ATs and fast times. Face it, if you could be reasonably sure your time would improve by 5 percent if you sculled in a green boat, green paint would be the hottest thing in boathouses since plastic boats.

GOING ANAEROBIC

When one "goes anaerobic," the lactic acid system kicks in, working alongside the aerobic system to provide the extra energy you are demanding. Since the lactic acid system does not use oxygen, lactic acid and carbon dioxide are produced as by-products. The lactic acid increases the acidity of the blood, while the carbon dioxide is carried back to the lungs where it is exhaled. So, two indicators of lactic acid system activity are increased acidity of the blood and an increase in the volume of carbon dioxide exhaled. Since both of these factors stimulate the breathing rate, you would also expect to see increased breathing rates when exercising at or above AT. Although this increased breathing rate is one way of determining AT, it's somewhat imprecise.

Although the lactic acid system is not using oxygen, in reality the use of oxygen does continue to increase when you cross the anaerobic threshold. Oxygen consumption just does not increase as fast as it did when you were getting the vast majority of your energy from the aerobic system.

Oxygen is required to remove lactic acid from the muscles and blood and convert it to glycogen and other substrates. This requirement for additional oxygen is referred to as oxygen debt. If you're exercising at an intensity above AT, your body is using all available oxygen to produce energy. You simply do not have the oxygen you need to pay off the oxygen debt until you stop exercising. Therefore, the buildup of lactic acid during anaerobic work means you will have to consume more oxygen after you have finished the work (and thereby reduced your muscles' demand for oxygen) to rid yourself of the lactic acid you built up during exercise. This heavy breathing after completing a high-intensity exercise bout also blows off the carbon dioxide produced by the lactic acid system.

There is substantial evidence that lactic acid accumulation in the body can have significant effects on performance and is one of the limiting factors in endurance sports. This is especially true for scullers due to their high reliance on the lactic acid system, particularly during the early stages of 2000 meter races. You may have experienced some of the effects of high acid levels before. When the blood's pH falls below 7, the nervous system becomes depressed and the individual can become disoriented and comatose. This may contribute to the rare-but-not-unknown occasion when a sculler passes out after, or during, a race or workout.

During your training schedule devote substantial time and effort to improving your ability to avoid producing lactic acid. Since you will have to produce some lactic acid if you want to go fast, you will also have to work on mitigating the effects the buildup of lactic acid may have on performance. Of course, the easiest way to avoid lactic acid build up is to remove the proximal cause by sleeping in.

NUTRITION

Athletes engaged in heavy training are burning between 45 and 87 kcals per day per kilogram of body weight. That's why they can eat doughnuts, power lunches, even dorm food, and still maintain a lithe and youthful figure. If you are rowing in cold weather, you may well be burning even more kcals. The fuel source for almost all work performed by humans is either fat, carbohydrate, or protein.

Fat, carbohydrate, and protein can all be used as a substrate for the phosphagen system because each can be used to recreate ATP. For the other anaerobic energy system, the lactic acid system, carbohydrate in the form of glycogen is the only possible fuel source. Fat is not a viable substrate for the lactic acid system since the breakdown of fat does not lend itself to short, intense exercise bouts.

The aerobic energy system is a little more flexible. Fats, protein, and carbohydrates can all be used as fuel sources. You don't have to rely on an adequate supply of one particular fuel source to produce energy aerobically. However, carbohydrates are the preferred fuel source and are most commonly used during exercise by the aerobic energy system.

Carbohydrate Metabolism

For scullers, the importance of carbohydrate (and the body's mechanisms for metabolizing carbohydrate) cannot be overstated. You store a lot more fat than carbohydrate, and fat contributes a lot of the energy used during longer events (50 percent to 90 percent of the energy used in an exercise bout lasting over 60 minutes comes from fat). But in shorter events, "carbos" will play a more important role than fats.

The higher the exertion level the greater the percentage of energy supplied by carbohydrate breakdown. At exertion levels below 95 percent of maximal oxygen uptake, both carbohydrate and fats are used as fuel. At levels above 95 percent, almost all energy is derived from carbohydrate.

Glycogen Depletion and Sparing

Carbohydrate is called glycogen when it is in a form usable by the muscle cell. It can be stored in the muscle cell itself, in the blood, or in the liver.

The average person maintains a store of about 400 grams of glycogen in the body's muscles, with an additional 80 to 100 grams stored in the liver. All this glycogen will yield between 104 and 120 moles of ATP, or enough to produce over 1000 kcals of useful energy. If you are exercising just below your anaerobic threshold and are in pretty good shape, your glycogen stores will be pretty much depleted after 90 minutes or so. If you are working out in hot weather, your muscles may use as much as 75 percent more carbohydrate than under more moderate conditions.

This depletion of glycogen during aerobic exercise occurs in sequence at three different rates. In the first twenty minutes of exercise you consume glycogen at a rapid rate, primarily by taking it from the muscle cell's own stores. If you are a well-conditioned sculler, this first stage will probably be shorter. After a steady state is achieved, you consume glycogen at a slower but steady rate if you maintain the same level of intensity. This stage continues until you have depleted almost all of your stores of glycogen, at which point the third stage begins. This third stage is marked by a decrease in the rate of glycogen depletion. This decreased rate may be partially due to the dearth of glycogen available; if there is little left, it is hard to use it very fast.

Glycogen depletion is one of several causes of fatigue. Unless you are sculling in a very long race or are suffering from severe glycogen depletion, it should not have much influence on the outcome of your race. Studies show that glycogen depletion does have a negative effect on maximal power output during intense exercise, but the negative effect is minor unless muscle glycogen levels were seriously depleted before the start of exercise.

Glycogen depletion is usually associated with fatigue when the athlete has been exercising (during that exercise session) at a level below his AT. At levels above AT, other factors, such as lactic acid accumulation and the attendant decrease in muscle and blood pH (i.e. the muscle and blood become more acidic), will stop the athlete long before his glycogen supply runs out. At these higher intensity levels, glycogen is consumed at a rapid rate; but a great deal of it remains even after an athlete is exhausted.

As a result of endurance training, the athlete has two significant advantages over the couch potato. First, the athlete can store up to two times more glycogen. Second, at the same absolute intensity level the athlete will use less glycogen. This is referred to as glycogen sparing and is probably due to the athlete's greater capacity to utilize fat as an fuel source. The more fat you can use, the more glycogen you can save for the sprint in the final stages of an exercise bout.

Replenishing Glycogen

There are three factors affecting the speed at which one replenishes one's glycogen stores. Diet is key. If you are not consuming carbohydrates (remember glycogen is a form of carbohydrate), you have nothing from which to make glycogen. In fact, a study conducted to analyze the speed of glycogen replacement found that after a group exercised to exhaustion, very little glycogen was restored after five days of a no-carbo diet. So, if you don't eat carbohydrates, your muscles won't get them.

On a diet high in carbohydrate it takes approximately 10 hours to significantly replenish depleted glycogen levels. This depletion can have a definite effect on your ability to successfully complete multiple daily workouts and often affects scullers trying to lose weight. If you don't have glycogen in your muscles, you will not be doing much sculling. Keep this effect in mind if you are dropping or even just watching your weight; your power output capabilities could be seriously impaired if you aren't intelligent about your weight maintenance program.

The type of exercise is also important to the speed of glycogen replenishment. If you are engaged in interval training, your muscle glycogen stores may be somewhat lowered after a workout but the liver's store of glycogen will be pretty much untouched. In addition, fast-twitch cells replace glycogen stores faster than slow-twitch cells, don't store as much glycogen to begin with, and are preferentially recruited during intense interval training. You will not have to replace glycogen stores in slow-twitch cells because they haven't been depleted. Complete glycogen replenishment takes less time after interval training than after steady-state exercise.

An additional factor may be self-selection; endurance athletes chose, and stay with, their sport partly because they are physiologically adapted for that sport. Part of this adaptation is the ability to store lots of glycogen. A highly trained endurance athlete's muscle can store two times the glycogen stored by the average, untrained American. This is probably due to the amount of exercise the athlete gets, which constantly depletes the glycogen stores. This constant loading and depletion of glycogen trains the cell to become more efficient in obtaining and storing glycogen.

There are two additional storage sites for glycogen, the liver and the blood. The liver acts as a glycogen reservoir to be tapped as muscle glycogen levels drop. Significant decreases in liver glycogen levels have been found in individuals deprived of carbohydrate for as little as 24 hours. Glycogen is delivered to the skeletal muscle via the blood, constantly resupplying muscle cells with fresh glycogen.

Fat Metabolism

The aerobic breakdown of fat is somewhat different from the breakdown of glycogen and has significant implications for your training.

Fat is used as an energy substrate at lower levels of exertion, and carbohydrate (glucose and glycogen) is used at higher levels. At rest two-thirds of the substrate used to produce energy is fat and the remaining one-third carbohydrate. Fat has two interesting characteristics. It produces substantially more energy per pound than carbohydrate. This higher energy value means fat is a good fuel source for long, steady-state training.

On the other hand, compared to carbohydrate, fat metabolism requires more oxygen to produce the same amount of energy. This need for additional oxygen limits the usefulness of fat as an energy source for high-intensity exercise.

The supply of fat is essentially unlimited but the ability of the muscle cell to use fat is not. The use of fat as a fuel source is determined by the duration and intensity of the exercise, the conditioning level of the athlete, and the athlete's diet.

Some fats, in the form of free fatty acids, are carried in the bloodstream and are more readily available than fat stored in adipose tissue (those rolls around heavy-weights' waists). These free fatty acids are the primary source of fat used during aerobic exercise. There is some evidence that aerobic training increases the amount of free fatty acids in the bloodstream, but the processes in which fat is broken down do not lend themselves to high-intensity exercise.

At intensity levels above 60 to 70 percent there is not enough oxygen present to break down much fat. And above 95 percent no fat is used. Thus, your use of fat is limited to relatively low levels of exertion.

Athletes with the proper type and amount of conditioning have an increased ability within their skeletal muscle to oxidize fat. This increased ability is a result of greater quantities of enzymes, a more efficient system for delivering oxygen to the muscle cells, and higher levels of certain types of fat that are readily broken down.

Finally, athletes who consume more fat use more fat. Perhaps they have always consumed fat in some quantity so their bodies have adapted to this consumption by developing the ability to metabolize fat. One study analyzed the effect of a high-fat diet on the endurance of trained cyclists. It was found that when the cyclists were given a high-fat diet over an extended period, they could exercise for longer periods than they could on their regular high-carbohydrate diet. However, when they were tested before their bodies had a chance to adapt to the high-fat diet, their performance was significantly worse than normal. This is nothing earth shattering. The human body is quite adaptable and can make the best out of whatever you feed it. Just don't change your diet the day before a race and expect to see better results.

For scullers competing in events less than 30 minutes long, efficient fat metabolism will not play a very significant role, but it's vital to your ability train longer and harder and recover faster to train again.

DIET

Don't worry, this isn't another incredibly involved discussion on the importance of eating right. If you're consuming the typical American diet, you are getting more than enough protein but should increase the amount of carbohydrate you are consuming and decrease the amount of fat—especially animal fat, because the normal American diet just is not healthy.

Sculling requires carbohydrates, and the more sculling you do, the more carbohydrates you need. Although fat tastes great and is quite useful as an energy source, unless you plan on doing a tremendous amount of sculling at quarter pressure, fats will not be an important contributor to your energy supply. Keep the amount of fat you eat to under 35 percent of your diet, especially if you have plenty of fat conveniently stored on your body right now.

Make sure you consume enough calories, especially during the summer when appetites tend to decrease and training gets more intense. If you are eating a well-balanced diet, you are probably wasting your money if you want to take vitamin supplements. The possible exception is Vitamin C. There is some evidence that endurance athletes require three to five milligrams per day per kilogram of body weight.

Women, especially lightweights, should make sure they get enough calcium and iron. Calcium is important to help prevent amenorrhea, and iron is an essential component of hemoglobin. If you lack calcium in your diet, your body will get it from your bones. Weak bones lead to stress fractures, including stress fractures of the ribs. If you lack iron, your blood's oxygen-carrying capacity may be reduced and your ability to go fast significantly impaired. Iron deficiencies can rob you of the physiological improvements you have been working so hard to obtain.

If you are one of the few people who actually eat right, keep it up. Your dietary habits are ensuring your glycogen levels are up where they should be, you are getting all your vitamins, and you're getting just enough protein to build those strong muscles.

Unless you are engaged in heavy weight training, you'll need only about 1.5 grams of protein per kilogram of body weight per day; anything over that serves no purpose. Most of the rest of your calories should be carbohydrate.

An entire industry has been formed around liquid glycogen replenishment drinks for consumption during long exercise bouts. Many of the manufacturers claim their particular concoction works better, faster, has more of a secret compound that's vital to your health, or just tastes better.

One of the keys to glycogen supply replacement during exercise is the rate of gastric emptying, or how fast glycogen replacement liquids leave your stomach. These concoctions cannot be absorbed by the stomach; they have to get into the intestine in order to get into the blood.

At one time it was thought liquid absorption was severely hindered by exercise, but recent studies have pretty much disproved this. In fact, up to a point, the rate of absorption of liquids may actually be accelerated during intense physical activity. The breakpoint seems to be at 70 percent of maximal oxygen uptake. Above that level some studies have indicated the rate of gastric emptying is reduced. However, gastric emptying still occurs at a rate fast enough to benefit you, even at high levels of exertion.

Other factors that may have some influence on the usefulness of liquid supplements are the rate at which they are absorbed into the bloodstream, the type of sugar in the drink, and the concentration of the sugar. These drinks contain fructose, glucose, and glucose polymers. Once absorbed into the bloodstream all of these sugars are converted into glycogen by the liver, so none has any clear advantage over the others after it gets into the bloodstream. In fact, probably the best fluid replacement drink for you is the one you like best.

These supplements are designed to compensate for glycogen depletion, but their main purpose (no matter what the marketing literature says) is the replacement of water lost during exercise. During heavy exercise in hot, humid conditions, you may lose two liters of sweat per hour. In reality, fluid consumption during exercise can only replace about half of that water loss. If you are not careful, even if you are drinking a lot of water, you can become dehydrated.

There has been quite a bit of research into the best pre-exercise meal and the optimal time to have that meal. The outcome of most of these studies has been that pre-event meals can be a significant help to the endurance athlete but probably do not have much of an effect, if any, on events lasting less than an hour. There is an exception to this rule, and it's for athletes racing more than one time in a day. Pre-event meals and supplements may improve your performance if you are sculling twice in the same day.

There is some controversy regarding when to eat the pre-event meal and what it should include. At one time it was thought meals containing fructose might be converted into glycogen faster than other carbohydrates, but recent studies have pretty much dispelled this rumor. In fact, fructose has been shown to elevate lactic acid levels, a potentially significant problem for scullers.

The latest word is the best time to eat a pre-event meal is about four hours before the event. It should be a light, simple carbohydrate meal, no huge stacks of pancakes washed down with biscuits and gravy.

The potentially positive effects of caffeine must be weighed against the proven negative effects if one is to make an intelligent decision to consume caffeine before sculling. Caffeine is a diuretic: it reduces the body's water content. As a stimulant it may also significantly impair one's ability to concentrate and remain calm and focused before and during an event. This psychological effect would most certainly outweigh any minor positive benefits of caffeine.

Caffeine's effects—both positive and negative—depend heavily on dosage. The average cup (6 ounces) of brewed coffee contains from 100 to 150 milligrams of caffeine, a cup of tea 30 to 75mg, and instant coffee 80 to 100mg. The effects induced by caffeine include increased body temperature, higher blood pressure, increased metabolism, and higher blood sugar levels. Caffeine also may be linked to a better ability to burn free fatty acids for energy, possibly improving endurance. However, the endurance-enhancing effects of caffeine are mostly related to an improved ability to utilize fat as an energy source. Since fat is of little use as an energy source during a sculling race of 1000, 2000, or even 5000 meters, don't drink lots of coffee and expect it to help much.

Too much caffeine can produce a headache, increased excitability, and other undesirable effects. If you are going to drink coffee or otherwise consume caffeine before an event or practice, consume no more than 250 mg (two cups of coffee) two hours before the event, and no more than another 250 mg right before the start. Don't be surprised if you are sitting on the starting line and your mind is filled not with thoughts of good technique, well-executed race plans, and medal acceptance ceremonies, but with an intense desire to find a floating port-a-potty.

Chapter Eight

Conditioning

he key to an effective and efficient training program is to design the program to incorporate technical as well as physiological training. Too many scullers concentrate almost exclusively on the physiological component of sculling, relegating technique work and drilling to the warm-up and long aerobic pieces. You will race as you train, so you'd better be thinking about your technique every second you're in the boat. Your mind isn't doing anything else while you're rowing pieces, and you sure don't want to allow your mind to focus on the pain levels you are proceeding through, so you might as well focus on your sculling.

PLANNING

If you scull for the sheer joy of it, terrific. Don't burden yourself with the need to rigidly follow a plan or workout schedule; it will only detract from the spontaneity of your exercise.

If you are planning on racing or want to improve your sculling, you need a plan; otherwise you'll never improve. You will work on one aspect of your sculling one week, then notice something else has gone awry, which you will then redirect your attention to. Once that is "fixed," you'll then read about the latest drill the national team is using, and for a few days you'll focus on that. Then one morning in the boathouse locker room someone will remark that they noticed a technical flaw in your stroke, which you will then proceed to work on until the next most important thing comes along. The end of the season will soon be upon you and you may or may not be sculling any better, but you will definitely be more frustrated. Understandably, because you have just wasted another season.

Even if you don't like the idea of planning—even if you have to force yourself to do it—do it. A week or so after the sculling season has ended, take up pen and ink (or log on to your PC) and write down what went wrong and what went right. Break your experiences and goals into three categories: technique, physical conditioning, and self-satisfaction. Self-satisfaction should include such things as placing in the top three in the local masters regatta or enjoying your sculling more. Technique might include any technical aspect of your sculling, such as the slow catch that you are less than satisfied with; or it might include something about which you feel particularly pleased, your drive, for instance. Physical conditioning issues might be a lack of upper body strength or an improved ability to hang in there in the last mile during a head race. Whatever it is, you have to somehow quantify it or qualify it. If you can't identify it, you won't know it when you get there.

A point of emphasis: Don't focus just on the negative. Make sure to document what went right about the season just finished so you can discern how you were able to make the improvements. This positive reinforcement can not only show you how to improve your less-than-perfect areas but is vital to your enjoyment of the sport as well.

Which leads us to the next absolute. You have to keep a log. No ifs, ands, or buts. Those who cannot remember the past are condemned to repeat it, so if you can't recall the factors and situations that resulted in your performance (or lack thereof), you won't know what you need to change to improve. Get one of those pocket calendars with a few lines for each day. Each day, whether you work out or not, write something down. By making this a part of your daily routine you'll be less likely to forget it. Keep the calendar in your nightstand, in your desk drawer at the office, or in your car's glove compartment—do you have anything better to do while sitting at traffic lights?

What you record is up to you. At a minimum, record your waking pulse, the time you began your workout, the details of your workout, and some indicator of your satisfaction with the workout. If it was on the water, record the conditions and any technical factors of note, as well as the mileage for the day and the total accumulated for the season. If you happened to do some competitive pieces, record your results, even if the pieces were merely a friendly brush with your teammates. Be sure to note any changes in rigging as well. If nothing else, the log will give you lots of interesting reading in your sunset years.

George Sheehan once said, "Everybody is an experiment of one." Think of your oversights and errors as part of a process. Sculling is not a trip to a destination, it is a constant process of minute improvements. When you consider it in this light, any problems you encounter or mistakes you make represent one additional step on the path.

Most of the scullers I've met in the last ten years or so address the problems or difficulties somewhat differently. The preferred approach seems to involve putting your head down and smashing it against a brick wall until you either break through (most unlikely) or give up. Since most boathouse walls aren't brick, the frustrated sculler substitutes a few more interval pieces or perhaps a couple of afternoon rows in addition to the six mornings a week and the evening sessions on the stadium stairs, in the weight room, or both.

This is really stupid. The only one who'll will benefit from this childish and self-defeating behavior is your competition. Your significant other will hate you, your co-workers will find you difficult to deal with, and worst of all, you'll start doubting yourself.

If you have been sculling on a regular schedule more than a few months, you are a dedicated and conscientious athlete. Sure, every now and then you sleep through the alarm or bag the last piece, but most of the time you have gotten the day's work done. Give yourself some credit every now and again and you'll be able to approach the frustrating times with a more positive attitude and a better chance of making those times short ones.

If you need more convincing, consider the opinion of two German sports medicine physicians. Their contention is that many training sessions are rather senseless: "The problem is that the body can tolerate much higher training loads than is advantageous for a performance." We scullers tend to believe that if a little is good, more is a lot better. Not true.

Once you have established a set of realistic goals, there are four factors you must consider when designing a training program to achieve those goals. The demands of the sport are one of these factors. If you want to go fast and perhaps win a race or two, you will have to scull well and produce lots of ATP. Second, there are a lot of minute elements that, when combined, add up to one's sculling. These elements, whether mental, physical, or emotional are unique to each athlete. The other two factors are the physiological principles discussed in excruciating detail in previous chapters and what you do when you are not sculling. The physiological principles are cold hard facts that don't change. To a large extent life outside of sculling is beyond your control, unless you are independently wealthy and have no significant other. These last two factors are pretty much set; anaerobic threshold is anaerobic threshold, and you may work 9 to 5, live 15 miles from a dock, and live in New Hampshire.

In *The Complete Sculler*, Richard Burnell put it very well when he said, "If the sculler is only to be satisfied with success, in terms of winning races, it is better to face the fact, at the outset, that this sort of success is only to be had if time and energy for the necessary training are available."

SELF-EVALUATION

The physiological demands of sculling are enough to make one take up golf. Sculling is ranked at or near the top of the list of the most physiologically demanding sports in terms of the amount of energy required to complete the event, whether it be the three-mile head race or the 2000 meters. Even this characterization is somewhat misleading for it fails to recognize the sudden demand for extremely high-energy output that occurs at the start of the event. No other sport begins with an all-out sprint, especially one utilizing most of the major muscle groups. While the negative effects of this initial burst of activity can be ameliorated somewhat by a properly executed warm-up, there is not much the sculler can do about the lactic acid load produced during the start. But that's what makes sculling so much fun.

Although many sports use a lot of muscles and some require similar levels of exertion, sculling is alone in the demands it places on all energy systems and all muscles. This demand is there whether you are aiming for the Worlds, the championship of the Crab Feast regatta, or just out for a row across the lake. Because sculling is a repetitive motion using major and minor muscles in the legs, buttocks, lower and upper back, stomach, chest, shoulders, and arms (not to mention the muscles of the face which are recruited for those awful grimaces you see on the videotapes), the body's total oxygen requirement is very high.

The physical requirements of sculling can be broken down into five basic areas. These categories include flexibility, power or strength, local muscular endurance, anaerobic fitness, and aerobic fitness. Flexibility is simply range of motion. A flexible sculler is able to reach full compression easily and without overstretching muscles or other connective tissue. Power may be defined as the movement of a mass over a certain distance within a certain period of time. Power is what you use to get the oars through the water. The more load you have on the oar and the faster you get it through the water, the more power you have. Local muscular endurance is defined as the ability to repeatedly perform a specific task while maintaining a high level of power. Aerobic fitness is the ability to perform work aerobically and anaerobic fitness is, you guessed it, the ability to perform work anaerobically. Most physiologists believe the maximal oxygen uptake level to be the true measure of aerobic capacity, and technically speaking it is. Our concern is not with technical accuracy but with faster sculling, so we'll define aerobic fitness as the most energy one can produce before going anaerobic (crossing the threshold into anaerobic respiration). Anaerobic fitness is the amount of work one can perform above anaerobic threshold before exhaustion.

FLEXIBILITY

There are a couple of flexibility tests that are particularly well-suited to sculling because they approximate components of the stroke cycle.

All flexibility assessments should be performed after a good warm-up. The first test is the traditional toe touch with a slight modification. Instead of standing on a flat surface, stand with your toes over the edge of a step. Keeping your legs straight, bend over and reach as far down as possible. If you can reach past your toes, you have a pretty flexible lower back, short legs and long arms, or some combination. If you can't reach your toes, you need a little extra work on loosening up the muscles of the lower back and buttocks.

The second test assesses ankle flexibility. The motion of the ankle joint is important to scullers because an inflexible ankle results in the heel lifting off the footstretcher at the catch. This puts you in a weakened position since you cannot drive off the whole foot.

To perform the test, sit in a boat with the footstretchers adjusted properly and slide forward to the catch position. Don't force your heels to stay down, just slide forward as you would normally while sculling. You want to simulate the movement used while sculling, not get the best test result. Your heels should not lift up more than a half inch; an inch at most.

STRENGTH AND POWER

Explosive power is largely a function of muscle fiber type. The higher the percentage of fast-twitch muscle cells, the more explosive power you have. Unfortunately, short of performing a muscle cell biopsy, there is no absolute method for assessing muscle fiber composition. The vertical jump test, when combined with a few other tests, should give you a fairly accurate indication of your dominant fiber type. Remember, one of the effects of a large volume of sculling over several years is that the fast-twitch cells begin to look a little more like slow-twitch cells and vice versa. However, it is unlikely that the overall percentage will change.

To perform the vertical jump test you will need a pencil and a tape measure. Stand perpendicular to an outside wall with your feet spread about shoulder width. With pencil held in the fist closest to the wall, reach up as far as you can and mark the wall. Then, without a running start, jump with both legs as high as you can, reach above your head and mark the wall with the pencil still clutched in your fist. Do this three or four times, resting between each attempt. When you think you have jumped as high as you can, measure the distance from the lower mark, that's the one you put on the wall when you were standing on the ground, and the highest mark. This is your vertical jump score.

Evaluating the vertical jump is somewhat inconclusive because there hasn't been a study directly linking vertical jump with muscle fiber type percentage. However, we can make a general statement about the results. If your jump is less than 12.5 inches for women (18 inches for men), you probably have a higher than average percentage of slow-twitch fibers. If your vertical jump score is above 15.75 inches for women or 24 inches for men, you have a higher than average concentration of fast-twitch fibers. Don't despair if your fiber type doesn't match that of Olympic scullers, just learn to take advantage of what you have. There is very little one can do to significantly improve vertical jump ability.

Upper body strength is particularly important to scullers due to the heavy loads placed on the upper body during the drive. One of the traditional weight-lifting positions, the row lift or bench row, should give you a pretty good indication of your upper body strength.

The bench row requires a strong, flat board supported far enough off the ground to allow you to lie face down on the board and still have enough clearance to extend your arms to grasp a barbell under the board. The barbell is raised off the floor and supported to give you enough room to grab the barbell and complete the row without the barbell hitting the ground.

To perform the test, lie on the board, drop your arms on either side to the bar, then bring the weight up until it touches the bottom of the bench. Warm up well, then keep adding weight until you reach your maximum. Lift with your arms and back only; keep your toes and chest on the bench at all times. Be reasonable and don't get yourself an eight-inch thick bench; the short-term mental gratification

Testing flexibility: Keeping your legs straight, bend over and reach down as far as possible.

The vertical jump: Don't move the leg closest to the wall before the jump. You may want to put chalk on your fingertips instead of using a pencil.

will be more than outweighed by the feeling that overcomes you when you get to the line and you know you haven't done the work. You'll be able to tell your relative strength, or lack of it, by comparing your lifts with others'. You can also compare your own progress on the bench row as your training progresses.

There are many other strength assessment techniques and protocols that may help you learn more about yourself as a sculler. Fortunately, there are many different types of weight-training equipment you can use to improve your strength. Include a test for leg strength in your portfolio of evaluation techniques. It should be simple and straight forward, such as a leg press on a Universal weight machine or a squat with a barbell on your shoulders.

LOCAL MUSCULAR ENDURANCE

Local muscular endurance is very important to your ability to scull well when you are nearing the end of a race course. If your preference is for long distance racing, it is even more crucial to your success. Keeping with the simple methods of assessment, two tests you may want to use to evaluate your present ability and track progress over time are the stair run and the bench row. Both are fine, traditional methods of evaluating sculling ability that give great satisfaction to the coach and cause great trepidation among scullers. Must be good.

The best type of stairs are the concrete seats found in old college football stadiums. If you can't get to a stadium or they won't let you in when you get there, find a long set of outdoor stairs, preferably straight. There should be at least 30 steps, and the more the better. Your first stair run of the season should be perfect for the first assessment. Warm up, then run up the stairs and walk briskly down, limiting your pause at the top and bottom to three seconds at most. You have completed the test when you can no longer run up the stairs, or when you can keep this up for 60 minutes.

The bench row: Bring your elbows by the body to mimic the sculling motion.

The "Exorcist" stairs near Washington D.C.'s Georgetown University, ideal for scullers.

A word of caution. The first stair run of the season can be exhausting. If you drove to the stairs in a car with a manual transmission, leave plenty of time for your legs to recover before heading out into traffic, as you may find it very difficult to hold in the clutch with jelly legs.

The timed bench row is a standard test for all national aspirants and for good reason. One of the problems many scullers had in years gone by was a lack of upper body strength. To remedy this situation, the test was incorporated in the standard national team test. The accompanying table is self-explanatory.

Timed bench rows.

Category	Time limit	Weight
Light women	7 minutes	60 lbs.
Women	6 minutes	70 lbs.
Light men	6 minutes	80 lbs.
Men	6 minutes	90 lbs.
Teen women	5 minutes	50 lbs.
Teen men	5 minutes	75 lbs.

The bar must hit the bottom of the bench and can rest on the floor in between pulls. The best strategy is to do the test as if you were in a race. Set a pace in your mind before you climb on to the bench and lift on that pace. Avoid fast and furious lifting early on; this prompts lactic acid build-up and makes it difficult to continue lifting past the third minute. Conversely, if you try to save it for the end, you may run out of time before you run out of gas.

Physically, sculling itself is a pretty good evaluation of local muscular endurance. But you are thinking about so many other things while sculling that a meaningful evaluation is difficult. The parts of the body that get the most tired are the ones that need the most work, if you are sculling correctly and using them correctly. Stick to the more objective analyses and you will be better off.

ANAEROBIC FITNESS

Anaerobic fitness is the ability to perform work above the anaerobic threshold. The basis for this test is simple: to evaluate the athlete's anaerobic energy production ability and, more importantly, the ability of the athlete to tolerate the by-products produced by the lactic acid system. This test is best performed after you have a good idea of where your anaerobic energy threshold lies. You will need to use a Concept II ergometer as a testing device.

After you know what your anaerobic threshold is, convert the score to watts and add 30 watts (50 if you are a really serious sculler) to get your target reading for the test. Then get on the ergometer and warm up well. Make sure you record the warm-up in your log so you can replicate it exactly for subsequent tests.

When you're sufficiently warmed up, hit the reset button and crank it up to the target reading. From there the test is very simple. Keep the reading on the ergometer within 10 watts of the target and have someone record the elapsed time and total work output (in watts or meters, whichever you prefer) when you can no longer hold the score.

The elapsed time is actually a crude means of quantifying your ability to tolerate the accumulation of lactic acid and other nasty byproducts of the lactic acid energy system. The total power output is an indication of the amount of power you can produce while operating at a very high intensity.

When you're tested in the future you'll find that your anaerobic threshold has increased, so your target reading will increase as well. Don't be disappointed if you don't seem able to increase your time to exhaustion very much; remember you are working at a higher overall level. You should be able to increase the total power output as you get in better shape, and as long as you follow your own test protocol you will be able to measure improvement. Remember, the point of all this is to get better, and this test will certainly help. The test isn't fun but it's very important. Don't rationalize your way out of it.

AEROBIC FITNESS

The best and most accurate way of measuring aerobic fitness is to hook the athlete up to a computerized, expired gas analyzer and heart-rate meter and have him scull at progressively higher workloads until exhaustion is reached. This test will give a highly accurate measure of an athlete's anaerobic threshold and maximal oxygen uptake. Unless you are a graduate student in exercise physiology, can weasel your way into some study, or are a viable candidate for the national team, you probably don't have access to such equipment. You can do just fine without it, and while you won't be able to compare actual oxygen uptake levels with your fellow scullers, you will have a very accurate picture of your aerobic fitness level.

For the test you will need a friend, a Concept II ergometer, and some method of measuring heart rate. The best way to measure heart rate is to use an electronic meter with a chest band that transmits to a wrist receiver. If you don't have access to such a device, you can try counting your pulse with your fingers on your carotid artery (the one in the right side of the neck), but your readings may be pretty inaccurate.

Put the heart-rate monitor on and place the receiver in a place where your friend can read the pulse. Warm up for ten minutes or so, again using your normal routine. Set the monitor in the erg so it reads power output in watts and begin the test by sculling for five minutes at 125 watts. Concentrate on getting as close to the target reading as possible every stroke. Record your pulse at the end of five minutes, increase the output by 25 watts every minute, and have your friend record your pulse in the last five seconds of each minute. Keep sculling until you can't go any further, then warm down slowly.

You will now have a piece of paper with two columns of numbers, one being power output in watts and the other your heart rate for that exertion level. It should look something like the following table.

Time	Watts	Pulse
5:00	125	128
6:00	150	137
7:00	175	145
8:00	200	154
9:00	225	162
10:00	250	170
11:00	275	178
12:00	300	185
13:00	325	189
14:00	350+/-	193
END	350	195

If you study the chart carefully, you can see that the heart rate increases in parallel with the workload up to the twelfth minute (300 watts). At that point the heart rate begins to slow its rate of increase significantly. This point probably indicates the anaerobic threshold.

The bunch of numbers seems to indicate an anaerobic threshold around 300 watts or a pulse of 185 along with a maximal output of around 350 watts at a pulse of 195. Using these numbers you can design a training program specific to your unique characteristics.

Coaches, national team selectors, and people who race on ergometers indoors most often use a different test protocol. The test favored by these folks is either a six-minute elapsed time test (how far you can go in six minutes) or a 2000 or 2500 meter test. These tests will not tell you anything about your anaerobic threshold, and if your purpose for testing is to learn how to go faster, then the progressively difficult test serves that purpose quite well, for it gives you information you can use to improve the specificity of your training program.

SPECIFICITY OF TRAINING

Several different tests are often used to measure oxygen uptake. Some use a treadmill or bicycle ergometer as the resistance device. Although these devices may be appropriate for testing runners, cyclists, or untrained civilians, they will not give you an accurate indication of your aerobic condition. The reason is specificity of training.

If you are primarily a sculler, your body is quite proficient at using oxygen while executing the sculling motion. It is not as proficient at running. Therefore, if you try to determine what your aerobic fitness is by testing your ability to run, (i.e., using a treadmill to test aerobic fitness), what you will get is a very accurate indication of your ability to use oxygen while running. This does you very little good because your goal is to go fast in a boat or on an erg, not on a track.

Specificity of training means that your body will adapt to the stresses of training by becoming better able to perform those specific movements used in training. In other words, if you run a lot to prepare for sculling, you will become a better runner but not necessarily a better sculler. Sure, your heart and lungs will become more efficient and you will increase the peripheral vascularization of your legs, but you are training the body to move in a certain set pattern (running) which in no way resembles the movement you want to improve (sculling).

The rule of specificity of training applies to everything you do: weight lifting, stair running, cycling, sculling, and any other training activities.

FLEXIBILITY

Flexibility is the aspect of conditioning scullers most frequently skip. Everyone knows they should do it and very few scullers really do. They think their time is better spent on some "more physical" activity. When scullers do find the time to stretch out, they usually do it very casually.

Flexibility is important because it helps relax muscles and lengthen tendons and connective tissue, reducing the chance of injury. Moreover, scullers with limited range of motion in a crucial area, such as the lower back or ankle, may not be able to row a full stroke. And, flexibility work is vital to the continued ability to scull into old age.

Stretching should be done both before and after a workout. It is best performed after a light warm-up, say five minutes on the ergometer. This warm-up heats up the muscles and makes them more receptive to stretching.

Start from the head and work your way down, using long, slow, non-bouncing stretches. Make sure you limber up the neck, lower and upper back, and ankles before you row and the major muscle groups afterward. Stretching after exercise is especially important when you begin a new cycle, add another type of exercise to your routine, or complete a particularly strenuous workout. Post-exercise stretching helps to relieve the pain and soreness you will feel 24 to 48 hours later.

Realizing that practically no one is going to spend the oft-cited 20 minutes stretching, settle on three or four stretches and make sure you do them each day. When you stretch, hold the position a little beyond your normal range of motion for 20 to 30 seconds and then release slowly. Don't bounce or overstretch—this will have the opposite effect and may injure the muscle as well.

STRENGTH AND POWER

Sculling is weight lifting in a sitting position. Considered in this light, it is not surprising that many competitive scullers have incorporated some kind of weight training into their conditioning program. Weight lifting, done correctly, can make a significant difference in a sculler's ability to move a boat. The key is to do it correctly.

Don't bother with weights unless you are going to use them to closely mimic the motions you will use while sculling. To be effective, the weight training must include lifts specific to the sequence of movements used in sculling, take the same amount of time, and follow the same range of motion. In other words, the lifts should closely resemble sculling. Of course the different parts of the stroke cycle can be worked on individually. You can use a leg press, bench row, back extension,

This stretch loosens the muscles of the upper back and the trapezius.

Use this to loosen tight ankles.

An excellent stretch for the lower back. Do this after a long row.

clean, squat, upright row, and any other lifts which meet these criteria. If you really want to, you can spend hours lifting, but you have to understand that unless the lifts are analogous to the sculling motion, your time invested will only help you when lifting refrigerators or posing at the beach. Not that these activities aren't worthy of hours in the weight room.

There is an exception to this rule that has to do with antagonist muscles. Muscles almost always occur in pairs, with one opposing the other. The biceps and triceps, the quadriceps and hamstring are two examples of these antagonist pairs. Problems can arise if one of the muscles becomes considerably stronger than the other. Muscle pulls, strains, and other injuries can occur because the body is out of balance. To avoid these horrible things, make sure you strengthen the opposing muscles as well as the sculling muscles.

Strength gains are best achieved by lifting very heavy weights a few times. If you are trying to build strength, do three to five sets of five to eight repetitions each. The first set should be at a lighter weight, and all subsequent sets should be to the point of muscle failure. It is important to reach this point since most of the improvements in strength occur as a result of the last few reps of each set. Don't lift to failure more than once a week.

If you don't have access to weights, you can use an ergometer to simulate weight training by putting the cable on the small sprocket, opening the vents all the way, and, as hard as you can, rowing five strokes on and fifteen off four or five times.

LOCAL MUSCULAR ENDURANCE

There are many ways to develop local muscular endurance (LME), the best of which is probably sculling. Unfortunately very long, exhausting pieces that happen to be best for developing local muscular endurance can also be bad for technique since the mind tends to leave the boat toward the end of the piece and technique falls apart. Fortunately you have other ways to improve your LME which will exhaust you without hurting your technique. Weight circuits are one of the most common LME training methods, yet they seem incredibly boring and pointless. I prefer running stairs and bench rows, although stairs and bench rows don't cover all the major muscles used while sculling; they do train the whole leg, buttocks, upper back, arm, and shoulder muscles. Stairs, whether they are stadiums or the "Exorcist" stairs in Washington, D.C., build great leg endurance. Again, make sure you are running them at the same speed you expect your legs to move when you scull. Bench rows are also quite simple. Do them in whatever sets you wish and keep a constant pace.

ANAEROBIC FITNESS

The best way to develop anaerobic fitness is interval training. Interval training is a method based on the progressive overload principle, a complex name for a relatively simple concept. Overloading is working at a level higher than you would during an event. For example, if you can row 2000 meters in 8 minutes flat, you might do intervals of one minute at a 7:30 pace. This fast pace helps you to become accustomed, both physiologically and mentally, to very high levels of exertion. Another advantage of interval training is it enables you to do a lot more work, albeit in smaller amounts, than you could if you rowed one continuous pace.

While intervals can help you become significantly faster, they can also burn you out if you are not careful. Many scullers tend to overdo interval training, perhaps because they believe anything that hurts that much must be good for them. I very clearly remember doing pretty intense interval work in March in preparation for the summer racing season. The result: I was fast in April and May but got progressively slower as the season approached. By the time Nationals arrived I was dead slow, exhausted, and hating life. Intervals can help you increase your anaerobic capacity significantly only if they are used appropriately.

Before you begin interval work you should have a solid aerobic base and a few hundred miles under your hull. This conditioning will reduce your chances of injury by preparing your muscles for high-stress work.

Interval Training

Interval training is best described by its terms.

Work interval: The distance, number of strokes, or length of time the interval is to be performed, e.g., 500 meters, 30 strokes, one minute.

Rest interval: The recovery period between intervals.

Work/rest ratio: The time ratio between the work and rest intervals, e.g., 1:2 means the rest interval is twice as long as the work interval.

Set: A group of work/rest intervals, for example, 6 x 1 minute on/1 minute off.

Repetition: The number of work intervals per set.

Percent effort: Relative to your best time over the distance you will be racing, e.g., 105 percent would be at a speed 5 percent faster than your speed over the course. Without a calculator in your boat, you can figure this out for yourself. Are you working a little harder or a lot harder than you would be during the race?

There are a few other general principles that apply to intervals. For example, since the purpose of interval training is to accomplish more work than you would be able to do in one continuous piece, make sure the rest interval is long enough to allow your breathing to slow to near normal and your heart rate to drop to 110 to 120 beats per minute. During the interval itself your pulse should reach your maximum or pretty close to it.

Your work load while in interval training should increase from week to week. Very intense interval training should follow several weeks of easier interval training. Try to maintain this maximal workload for no more than a couple of weeks. Because intervals should be very intense and very stressful, you will need a lot of rest between interval training days—at least 48 hours and perhaps more if you are tired, sick, or think you may be overworking. In any case do not do more than three hard interval workouts per week, and only if you are within six weeks or so of the key event in your sculling schedule. Be sure to drastically reduce the workload a week before your main event.

You must stretch and warm up and warm down thoroughly when you are doing intervals. This will not only reduce the amount of post-exercise trauma and pain you will experience but also hasten your recovery.

AEROBIC FITNESS

Once you have determined your anaerobic threshold (AT) and maximal oxygen uptake (as measured by power output on the ergometer), you can design a program to increase both of these critical measurements. To improve maximal oxygen uptake you should include both long, slow distance sculling pieces (LSD) of at least 20 minutes each and shorter pieces of somewhat higher intensity, say ten beats below your anaerobic threshold, with a minute or two of rest between each piece. The LSD work will help increase peripheral vascularization so your muscles are better supplied with nutrients and oxygen. The higher intensity pieces will also help increase cardiac output because your muscles will be demanding larger quantities of oxygen.

One higher intensity workout is 20 strokes on, 5 strokes off for some extended length of time, say 25 minutes. This enables you to work hard and rest before you build up any lactic acid.

At least once a week go out for a very long, steady piece. You can do this on your bike, on the erg (boring!), in the boat, or wherever you are sure you will get the work in. Ideally, the piece should be at least twice as long as the other LSD pieces in your schedule. A bike ride works well because once you are an hour away from home you have no choice but to ride home. You may also try rowing on an erg during the entire first half of a football game, but make sure you aren't sculling poorly or bad technique will be deeply imbedded in your muscular memory.

Anaerobic threshold work should be done at a heart rate as close to your AT as possible. A classic AT workout is 3 × 20 minutes with several minutes rest between each piece. If that seems a little unreasonable, try 3 × 15, 2 × 20, or a decreasing pyramid of 20 minutes, 15, and 10. One AT workout I like is 5 × (8 minutes on, 2 minutes off) at AT. The important thing is to do the AT work at least two times per week in the off season and once a week during the season.

Make sure you retest your AT every six weeks or you'll find your AT work is not at AT because you are in better shape.

TRAINING PROGRAMS

There are three principles upon which to base a conditioning program. The first is specificity of training. As discussed above, you row as you train. When you develop your training program, remember the things that will make you a better sculler are going to resemble sculling pretty closely. The second principle comprises the four basic components of an exercise program: frequency, duration, intensity, and type. Frequency refers to how often you exercise as well as how many pieces you may do during a particular workout. Duration is simply the length of the entire workout or individual piece. Intensity is how hard you work during that piece. Type is the type of exercise you perform in general, such as aerobic or high-intensity anaerobic, as well as the mode of exercise, e.g., cycling, running stairs, or sculling. The other principle or concept is the cycle.

There are two basic types of cycles. A "micro" cycle is a series of workouts of varying intensity performed over a certain period, usually a week, or month. The purpose of this type of cycle is to allow the sculler to work hard, recover, and work hard again while minimizing the chances of overwork and burn-out. The "macro" cycle is simply the training plan for the year. The purpose of the macro cycle is to allow the sculler to concentrate on different aspects of a conditioning program, with each aspect building on the work done before. A very basic macro cycle might include work in the off-season on technique and aerobic conditioning and work in-season on speed.

Each cycle should have a primary goal and one or two secondary goals. Your first cycle in November and December might emphasize maximal oxygen uptake and strength conditioning. The second cycle in January and February would emphasize AT and strength, with continued aerobic fitness work as well as LME work in February. March would be a transition month with continued AT emphasis but a switch to LME work in the weight room and the introduction of some shorter, more intense work once or twice a week.

April's emphasis might be more race-specific, with longer intervals, including lots of five-minute pieces. These longer intervals could be interspersed with LSD and AT work, although the pieces would be shorter and a little more intense. May would emphasize anaerobic fitness training, with a gradual increase in intensity. Strength training should be continued during these months.

June and July are the competitive periods, with the emphasis on race-specific preparation and simulation. Lots of lactate tolerance pieces, which are short (45 seconds), very intense pieces followed by longer periods of rest. The interval work may be combined with LSD work to help the recovery process and emphasize technique, which occasionally suffers as a sculler tries to force up this rating.

The racing season is not the time to pile on lots of work. In fact, you can cut back on the workload by as much as 60 percent as long as you maintain the intensity. This reduction will not hamper your conditioning if you have a good base, will help you maintain a peak longer, and will prevent burn-out.

The first part of August also is a competitive period, but you should de-emphasize any large quantity of hard work. You aren't going to get in any better shape and your risk of overtraining is pretty high. Do a hard piece every other day, enjoy your sculling, and get ready for your well-earned vacation from sculling.

The fall season may include head races every other week, so the training emphasis is on maintaining conditioning for the races by doing long interval work and improving on the technique problems you identified at the end of the summer.

If you want sample workouts for each month you can subscribe to the USRA's athlete newsletter. The workouts it includes are for potential candidates for the national team. With what you've learned you can certainly design a schedule more appropriate for you, your goals, and your strong and weak points. Don't do national team workouts just because the national team does them, do them because they make sense based on your unique situation. What follows is a sample conditioning program to integrate these components and produce a plan designed to enable a mythical sculler to accomplish his goals. Any resemblance to any sculler you know is purely coincidental.

SAM'S CONDITIONING PROGRAM

Sam is a master sculler with a non-sculling wife and child. Sam has been sculling competitively for several years and wants to move up a notch or two. He has never really sat down and thought about his goals, except for the usual daydreaming in the car on the way to work. This year is different; Sam did pretty well at a couple of area regattas and wants to go to the Nationals next year. So he's decided to get serious and plan his campaign.

Sam has decided his goal next summer is to place in the top three in his age category in the single at the National Championships. He hopes to win the masters single at the Head of the Hamonassett regatta ten weeks after the Nationals. Several local scullers he knows from local regattas went to the Nationals this year and did well; Sam won more than he lost against them so he feels his goals, while not easy, are certainly within his grasp. To reach those goals, Sam knows he will have to improve his sculling technique considerably. He tends to hang at the catch and not on the drive, so he knows if he can improve his technique alone, he will be more efficient and faster.

His work schedule and family obligations pretty much limit him to early-morning workouts, but very near the office is a gym with weights and a couple of ergometers. The gym opens at 6:30 a.m.

Before he can get started on his training program, Sam decides he has to find out what kind of shape he is in. Since the season ended just a week ago, he figures he is in top shape, so the tests should be revealing. They are.

Sam finds out that his upper body strength and endurance are not great. The results of his anaerobic power tests are pretty good, but his anaerobic threshold tests shows his AT is only about 72 percent of his maximal effort. He also discovers he has poor ankle flexibility.

Consider Sam's technical problems in light of his physiological test results. Sam has problems hanging on the oars through the drive. This is not surprising since his upper body strength and endurance are not what they should be. This is a chicken-and-egg problem: he may be weak because he doesn't hang on the oars or he may not hang on the oars because he is weak, especially at the end of the piece. Upon further reflection, Sam recalls that he almost always lost ground in the last 500 meters of the race. Sam's poor ankle flexibility may account for part of this problem. Sam can't press his entire foot into the footstretcher, which makes it hard to feel the connection between the footstretcher and the oar handle, which comes from hanging on the oar.

Sam now knows what he must do to accomplish his goals. He has to improve his technique at the catch and during the drive while continuing to scull well on the recovery. He has to increase his anaerobic threshold and local muscular endurance, especially in the upper body. Finally, he has to get more flexible, both to improve his sculling and to minimize his chances of injury.

Sam rows the fall season with an emphasis on hanging on the oars throughout the drive. He also makes sure he stretches before each row. When the ice hits the water, Sam heads indoors to begin the December/January cycle of once-a-day workouts featuring upper body strength training and AT work. He tests his AT again in the middle of December and at the end of January.

February includes more AT work along with timed bench rows and more weight lifting focusing on explosive power. Sam continues his stretching because he is doing work he hasn't tried before and he is leery of injury.

In March Sam is once more on the water, but this year instead of doing the same thing everyone else is, Sam concentrates on his technique and AT work, which showed a lot of improvement in the test he did the first of the month. This emphasis is continued until the beginning of April, when Sam starts to increase the intensity a little by doing some long (10-minute) intervals twice a week. He still does his AT work once a week and LSD on the other two days. Saturday is for weights; Sam wants to maintain his hard-earned strength improvements.

In the middle of May Sam begins interval training twice a week, starting off with relatively easy workloads. His buddies are beating him easily in the weekly 2000 meter row, but Sam is unconcerned because he is understroking them by four strokes.

His work starts to pay off in June. He is still fresh and looks forward to sculling every morning even though the intervals are getting a little more intense. He is aiming for the Nationals the first weekend in July, so he really cuts back on his workload the last week in June.

On the long drive to the Nationals Sam reviews his progress. He is sculling much better, with little hang at the catch and lots of hang on the oars during the drive. He feels prepared for the Nationals because he can row much harder and much longer before feeling the effects of lactic acid build-up. He is a little apprehensive about his late start on interval training because he will be racing 1000 meters, but still feels more prepared than ever for the upcoming race.

Sam wins the race, gets interviewed by ESPN, and by the time the Hamonassett rolls around he's a figure of respect among his fellow scullers.

Overtraining

Consider what could have happened had Sam not thought out his training program. Overtraining is a phenomenon caused by overstressing the athlete physically or mentally. Although stress is an integral and ever-present part of training, too much stress or the wrong kind can result in the protective response known as overtraining. Interestingly, overtraining occurs most often in highly motivated, self-coached athletes as well as those coached by overly enthusiastic amateurs.

Overtraining can be brought on by frequent competition, abrupt changes in the weather, a change in diet, or other sudden changes in a sculler's routine. Perhaps the most frequent cause is too much interval work too soon or without a sufficient aerobic base. In the haste to go fast some scullers try to squeeze out all the speed they can in the early spring, leaving them nowhere to go but slow when the racing season rolls around.

Overtraining is a very individual problem. Symptoms may include fatigue, a tendency to tire easily, loss of appetite, difficulty sleeping, and weight loss. The latter is perhaps the most common symptom, so make sure you record your weight each day if you think you may be at risk of overtraining. Physiological indicators of overtraining include a rise in resting heart rate and blood pressure and an increase in performance times. Among younger scullers the best symptoms are physiological indicators such as resting pulse; older scullers may know they are overtraining when their performance drops off and/or they develop colds or headaches. These symptoms are simply the body telling you it is time to take a break because the body can no longer handle the stress placed on it.

One cautionary note. A lack of motivation is often a symptom of overtraining, but only if it is a real symptom and not just an "I don't want to do five-minute pieces today" problem. If the lack of motivation lasts more than a few days and you have been doing the work up until then, chances are the symptoms are valid.

Treatment is complete rest. Not cutting back to half the workout or even just a technique row. You'll get a lot better a lot faster if you bag sculling entirely for a while.

The key to enjoying your sculling is to understand what you want to accomplish and what you need to do to accomplish your goals. From there it is up to you to determine how you will accomplish them. You are the only one who really knows how to make you fast. Take the science and apply it to you, and you will be successful.

Chapter Nine

Common Sense and Safety

culling may well be the least hazardous thing you do all day. If you have even a little common sense you will be able to scull for years without incurring anything more serious than an occasional bruised ego. That may be the most severe of all sports injuries, but it is a lot less expensive to fix than a torn medial collateral ligament.

Sculling is safe because it is not a contact sport, does not require you to carry your own weight while exercising, and allows you to set your own pace. People only run into health problems when they are doing something they know they shouldn't, like interval training in July in Philadelphia at 2 p.m. during a smog alert, or sculling blades squared with eyes closed in March in Chicago. In other words, when they do things common sense tells them they shouldn't.

For scullers common sense is often overmatched by strong obsessive/compulsive tendencies. These tendencies result in scullers doing things they really know they shouldn't do but feel compelled to because if they don't, they are not dedicated enough. You have to be smart enough to know when a situation is unsafe or potentially unsafe and wise enough to remove yourself from such a situation.

WHERE TO SCULL

If you are a novice sculler or have never sculled on a particular body of water before, ask the natives if there are any peculiarities about the area, people, water quality, or whatever before launching. Then act upon your knowledge. The first time you head out, stop and look around every so often to get a sense of the area, identify local landmarks, and plot your course from there. Don't scull with your head down and your gaze fixed on your stern.

If you row in a city, ask other people around the boathouse if there are any potential problem areas you should be aware of. Each area has its own unique problems: the dam at Boathouse Row in Philadelphia, the freighters in Long Beach, the wakes from coaching launches in Boston, and manatees in the rivers of Florida. Educate yourself and be alert and you'll improve your chances of avoiding difficulties.

Although each body of water has its own idiosyncrasies, there is a prescribed traffic pattern and set of rules for all bodies of water. Powerboats must give way to human-powered craft and everyone must give way to sailing vessels. On most rivers the traffic pattern is the same: keep to your left (as you are sitting in the boat) heading upriver and down. Some folks get confused because they are sitting "backwards" in a shell; so to rephrase the directive, no matter what direction you are heading keep close to the land on your starboard side.

The pattern is reversed in Philadelphia, so don't be alarmed. They just do things differently in Philly.

Traffic patterns are not cast in stone. On occasion you may have to row up the wrong side of the river, perhaps when a regatta is being run or when a sudden thunderstorm blows in. In this case, be very careful and turn around every five or ten strokes to make sure there is no one in the way and that you are headed in the right direction. Things can look very different from the other side of the river.

If there is bridge construction or repair in progress, be very careful when approaching and sculling through. The construction crews will often change the traffic patterns on the river (if they even know there is traffic on the water) as they work their way across the bridge, so check for any indication of changes in the arches you are supposed to use. Don't feel safe if the underside of the bridge is draped with screens or tarpaulins to catch construction debris. During the recon-struction of Key Bridge across the Potomac River large chunks of bridge periodically fell into the river. One small rock actually punched a hole through the deck of a shell just feet from the woman in the boat.

Don't row blindly. If you have to cut a piece short or stop sculling to check the situation out, do so.

Most sculling is done on inland, linear bodies of water such as rivers, reservoirs, and long lakes. These linear bodies lend themselves to a uniform traffic pattern. Some of you more adventurous types may scull on open lakes and perhaps even the ocean or parts thereof where the traffic pattern may be somewhat more freeform. The only thing that is uniformly consistent is the apparent right-of-way held by water skiers over all other modes of transport. Know the area before you launch.

If you scull in an area where there are other scullers or high school, college, or club crews cluttering the water, you should know the etiquette for passing. The overtaking sculler should make it clear on which side he wants to pass. This can be done by verbal or other means, such as overtly and very obviously pointing your bow in the direction you wish to go. The boat that is being overtaken should yield. If this is not possible or if you are unsure of the intentions of the overtaking boat, don't be shy. Get the sculler's attention and ask for clarification.

Keep your head up, especially when you're tired, and securely fasten your safety light.

If the overtaking boat has a coxswain, don't assume he sees you. Make sure to attract the attention of the bowman, the coxswain, or both. This is especially important if there are several crews out and they appear to be novices, since the coxswains may be paying more attention to each other than to navigational hazards such as yourself. The same rule applies to coaches, who are often so intent on observing their crews they neglect to look where they are going.

When you yield to an overtaking boat, make sure you aren't pushed into the shore. You will probably be bounced around in a wake for a few strokes, which can be quite annoying. Try to maintain your composure and scull through it. The world is full of nice, well-intentioned people who just don't think about the implications of their actions. Scullers just seem to encounter more of them than other athletes do.

WHETHER TO SCULL

When to row is often a difficult decision. With the pressures of school, work, family, and social life all making demands on one's time, sculling has to fit in around other plans. Your best bet is probably first thing in the morning. If you leave it until the afternoon or early evening, you'll find that other things just seem to keep cropping up and taking over your workout time. Not a whole lot comes up at 6 a.m.

In the summer the sun is up early enough to eliminate the need for lighting on a boat, but in the early spring and fall you may find some or all of your workout is done in darkness. For safety purposes you should wear light-colored clothing. By the same token, dark clothing helps others see you in bright, sunny conditions, especially if the sun is low on the horizon and there is a lot of glare off the water.

If you think you are likely to encounter low-visibility conditions, put a light in your bow to warn other boats of your approach. You may also want to put a red light somewhere on the stern. If you do put a light in the stern, shield it with aluminum foil or something else to prevent its shining toward you and interfering with your vision.

Lights should be waterproof and bright enough to be seen at some distance, say a quarter-mile. The best type of light for the bow is the type used by ground crews at airports. It has a translucent yellow, orange, or light green cone over the bulb end of the light that allows it to be seen from all directions. Keep a spare set of batteries for each light in your locker or car; the day the light burns out is the day you will need it.

Remember to look around every few strokes. An alternative to glancing over one's shoulder is a mirror attached to a headband or glasses. The mirror acts as a front view mirror. Scullers who use this device swear by it, but I could never get comfortable with it. If you can get used to watching the horizon bob up and down as your head moves and if you can remember that you are looking at a reversed picture, then a mirror will make your sculling safer.

Some people scull with headphones on as they listen to music or tapes on sculling technique. A terrible idea. If you want to listen to sculling technique tapes then do so on the ergometer, not in a boat where you are putting yourself and others at risk because you cannot hear what is going on around you.

SWIMMING, AND THE AVOIDANCE THEREOF

Swimming is the only other athletic skill you'll find necessary, and you will find it necessary. There are only two types of scullers: Those who have flipped and those who are going to flip. Since you know you'll go in sooner or later, you should know how to swim when the inevitable occurs.

So the inevitable occurs and you go in. First, don't panic. Your body's natural reaction is to gasp as the cold water hits your body; try to keep your mouth shut when you start to slide in. Second, don't fight it. You may well damage the boat if you valiantly try to stay vertical in spite of an overwhelming force inclined to prevent this. A dunking is usually slow-motion; one side of the boat dips down, you start to slide out over the gunwale, your feet come out, the boat capsizes, and you're in the water frantically trying to prevent your favorite sweatshirt from becoming a part of the muck below. After you rescue your beloved apparel, you have to get back in the boat.

The best option is to swim the boat to shore, empty it, and climb back in from a rock or shallow beach. If the water is not cold and you aren't too far from shore, try this. It minimizes your chances of damaging the boat. Make sure the fin is well clear of any rocks before you try to climb back in.

If it is cold or you are too far from shore, you can get back into the boat from a dunking. The rule is "any way you can is fine," but there are a couple of things to keep in mind if you wish to minimize damage to your beloved craft. Hold both oars in one hand, preferably near the handles. The blades should be flat on the water. Place the other hand between the track toward the bow and throw a leg over the bow. You are now lying on top of the boat, with one hand still firmly gripping the oar handles. Slowly sit up, place your free hand behind you where it can do the least damage and scoot your rear end into the seat, leaving your feet in the water to aid your balance. Finally, lift your feet into the boat and slide them into the shoes. This is a pretty ungraceful maneuver. Try to be as gentle as possible throughout to reduce damage to the boat as well as chances of a repeat of the original miscue.

Whatever you do, don't abandon the boat. Your chances of making it safely back to the dock are greatly enhanced if you can use the hull as a life preserver, and you'll get back a lot faster if you can scull back.

WEATHER

Your biggest health risks will be related to weather. Cold, heat, storms, fog, and pollution all pose special hazards to scullers.

Cold

Dress warmly but in layers so you can strip down as you warm up. Make sure to put the layers back on as you cool down so you don't get chilled. The first layer should be made of one of the wicking-type fibers such as polypropylene or Thermax. These fibers do an excellent job of transporting moisture from the body to the outer layers, where it can evaporate. If you use cotton as an inner layer, you'll find your sweat stays close to you and you get chilled quickly when you stop exercising or turn around into a headwind.

For the outer layer, use wool or other clothes that will retain heat even if wet. Polarplus and other fleece variants dry very quickly. Your outer layer should be easily removed as you get warmed up.

I don't recommend the traditional rowing jackets made of nylon or other "waterproof" materials because they rarely are completely waterproof and they retain a lot of moisture. Since you heat up quickly and put out a lot of heat (and sweat) while sculling, they really don't seem to serve much of a purpose. You won't wear this type of jacket much beyond the warm-up or you will be swimming in sweat before the first piece is over. If you are wearing such a jacket for warmth, you might be better off with something that gives you protection from the wind yet breathes.

Some manufacturers have come out with Gore-Tex versions of the rowing jacket, which is a little better since it breathes and definitely is waterproof. However, it does not breathe enough to keep you dry if you are sculling hard in moderate temperatures. Life is full of trade-offs; you either can have a waterproof jacket or you can have one that breathes quite well, you cannot have both unless you buy two jackets.

A light nylon windbreaker that's been treated with a water-repellent coating keeps most of the backsplash off you and will even keep you dry in a light rain. It also breathes very well. Columbia, North Face, REI and other outerwear manufacturers make such garments. Make sure you get one that gives you lots of mobility and covers your arms and wrists even when you are fully compressed at the catch. Also, make sure the tail isn't too long or it will get caught in the slide. If you scull north of Florida or Mission Bay, you'll get a lot of use out of this jacket—so buy a good one.

Some scullers are too macho to use pogies (big mitts that fit over the oar handle and the hand). Except in extreme weather you'll want to take them off during or just after the warm-up, but they will prevent that awful pain in the hands that comes when you thaw out after an initial freeze.

In really cold weather you'll find your hands warm up a lot faster if you keep your oars in a warm area. The reason cold-weather sculling is so hard on the hands is your hand has to warm up the oar handle before it can stay warm itself. If possible, store your oars in a heated area such as a locker room or repair room to reduce your discomfort.

Some scullers use a shorty wetsuit in early spring and late fall as an insurance policy in case they go in. If you do choose to use a wetsuit, remember it will only improve your chances in the event of immersion; it will not guarantee safety. Be cautious.

The biggest problem with winter sculling is the risk of cold-water immersion, also known as flipping. If you find yourself in the water with no one around to help, you'll be suffering from hypothermia unless you can get out of the water very quickly. Since water conducts heat 25 times faster than air, you get cold fast.

Scullers have additional problems associated with cold-water immersion due to the nature of their activity. If the sculler has been rowing fairly hard, the blood vessels near the skin are probably open (dilated) to allow for heat dissipation and nutrient and blood supply to the working muscles. The cold can cause the blood vessels to dilate even further, hastening heat loss. Older scullers and scullers with cardiovascular problems should make an extra effort to avoid cold-water immersion.

The basic rule for survival is to conserve heat. No matter where you fall in or how cold the water is, get out as soon as possible. If you can't get in the boat, crawl up on the hull of the boat, getting as much of your body out of the water as possible. You can kick it to shore from there. Don't worry about damaging your boat, this is a matter of survival. In your effort to save the boat, you may well end up harming yourself. If for some reason you cannot get out of the water, at least keep your head and neck out to conserve what heat you can. In any event, keep your clothing on; it will help to slow the rate of heat loss.

Unless you are very close to shore, don't try to swim and push the boat in. Swimming in cold water burns additional calories and increases the rate of heat loss.

Once back at the dock get out of the boat and into a warm area as fast as possible. Don't worry about the boat; you can always go back and put it away later or someone else can take care of it for you. Take off all your clothes, get into a warm (not too hot) bath or shower, and drink warm liquids.

If you encounter someone else who looks as if they are a victim of hypothermia, do not be dismayed if they appear to be dead. In fact, the symptoms of a successful adaptation to cold-water immersion are very close to those of death. This adaptation is known as "mammalian diving reflex."

Mammalian diving reflex is the body's way of decreasing circulation to the periphery of the body to help maintain a warm environment for the vital organs in the body core. The victim may appear to have a bluish tinge to his skin, no pulse or respiration, dilated pupils, and be completely unresponsive. If the victim has these symptoms, you must start CPR immediately, even if the victim has been in the water for an hour.

If you do not start CPR, the victim will certainly die. If you do start CPR, there is a chance he will live. You may have to continue CPR for an hour or so before you can be sure there is no chance of reviving the victim; if you are not sure he is beyond hope, he probably isn't; so wait for a medical professional before ceasing CPR.

In any event, if the victim is incoherent, unconscious, or irrational, call an ambulance while you start the rewarming process. Don't listen to protests; if you think the person may be in danger take it upon yourself to seek help. Hypothermia is serious and can be deadly if not recognized and treated promptly.

Heat

Heat, especially when combined with high humidity, can be just as deadly as cold. It is also harder to diagnose some heat-related maladies, so heat may actually be a bigger risk than cold. The risk increases if a sculler has not had time to acclimate himself to hot weather or if he is dehydrated. Heat-related disorders range in severity from cramps to heat stroke.

Heat cramp.

Heat cramps occur primarily in healthy, well-acclimatized athletes. These athletes may get cramps in their legs and back an hour or so after exercising. Such cramps are believed to be caused by an insufficient amount of sodium (salt) in the diet; treatment is consumption of sodium and a lot of water. However, do not consume sodium salt if any symptoms of heat exhaustion are present.

Heat syncope.

Heat syncope, or fainting, can be brought on by a combination of blood pooling in the lower extremities due to vasodilation and fluid loss due to sweating. The result is a decreased return of blood to the heart and a resulting drop in blood pressure. This drop in blood pressure may be accelerated, deepened, or both by the chemical changes in the body due to loss of potassium from sweating. When all these horrible things occur, the athlete's brain does not get sufficient oxygen, leading to severe dizziness or fainting. Usually this spell is a brief one, but it may be a warning that the athlete's potassium levels are seriously depleted.

Rest and fluid replacement are the recommended treatment, along with potassium replenishment. If you are an older sculler, you would be well advised to take a few days off, tell your doctor what happened, and eat lots of bananas.

Since heat syncope may be a sign of serious potassium depletion, don't take any sodium or salt tablets if any symptoms of heat syncope are present, or if you even suspect a symptom is present. Sodium and potassium must be in balance if the heart muscle is to function properly; any significant imbalance could cause serious problems.

Heat exhaustion.

Heat exhaustion is even more dangerous than heat syncope. It is potentially life-threatening, even for young, healthy, acclimatized athletes. Symptoms range from the subtle—poor performance and emotional abnormalities; to the more obvious—cramps along with nausea, vomiting, headache, clammy skin, low blood pressure, heart rate, and extreme weakness.

Again, low potassium levels and the resulting sodium-potassium imbalance are heavily involved. However, the problem of low potassium is exacerbated by the athlete's acclimatization. The acclimatization results in the athlete developing an improved ability to retain sodium. When he sweats and urinates he is losing potassium just as he always did, but because he is more able to retain sodium his system is out of balance. Obviously the consumption of sodium, such as salt tablets, is going to cause serious problems since it worsens an already bad condition.

Victims of heat exhaustion should be taken to a hospital emergency room immediately. Do not allow the sculler exhibiting the symptoms described above to head home, to the office, or classroom. Heat exhaustion kills a lot of people every year because the victim and others don't take it seriously.

Heat stroke.

The most deadly type of heat-related disorder is heat stroke. Even if a victim is treated in a hospital emergency room or intensive care unit, he will most likely die.

Heat stroke's symptoms arise suddenly and catastrophically. Symptoms include seizures, heart failure, kidney failure, coma, and bleeding, among others. Not surprisingly, these events are related to potassium depletion. There is not much you can do for someone suffering from heat stroke. Prevention is the best way to deal with it.

Preventing heat stroke is no different from preventing any other heat-related disorder. Make sure you maintain the proper potassium-sodium balance, drink lots of fluids, don't take salt tablets, and do not try to make weight by sweating it off in a sauna or taking diuretics.

Humidity plays a very important role in heat-related stress because high humidity levels prevent the dissipation of heat through the evaporation of sweat. In conditions of high humidity, say 80 percent relative humidity and higher, you should be careful when the temperature is above 80 degrees Fahrenheit.

A very unscientific but quite useful formula for determining when conditions are unsafe for anything other than a technique row at quarter pressure is to multiply the temperature by .66, the humidity by .33, and add the two numbers together. If the total is over 82, bag the hard part of the workout; if the total is over 85, stay off the water entirely. Although this formula is by no means precise, it errs on the side of caution. Still, be even more cautious if you do not tolerate heat well or it's the first hot day of the year.

To make sure you understand this advanced math, here's an example. Say it is July in Omaha and you are heading out for your morning workout. The temperature is 88 degrees (you should have gotten out of bed earlier) and the humidity is 70 percent. Eighty-eight times .66 is 58, and 70 times .33 is 23. When you add 58 and 23 you get 81, so you could scull in this weather. You may not want to and you should not think less of yourself or anyone else if they choose to save it for another day. Also, remember it is more humid on the water so you may want to fudge the humidity numbers up a little bit to compensate.

So what do you do if you live in Miami and want to scull in the summer. First, try to scull in the coolest part of the day, the early morning. Second, consume lots of potassium. If you get too much, you'll just pee it away. Third, drink lots of water, electrolyte replacement fluids, or both and drink them constantly, especially while on the water. Fourth, get acclimatized by sculling gently the first few days of hot weather to give your body a chance to adapt. Fifth, wear light-colored, loose-fitting clothing and take it off when it gets soaked since it keeps you hot when it is wet. Sixth, on really bad days put the erg indoors and pretend it is snowing outside. You are in Miami, so you'll have to pretend very well.

Individuals with cardiovascular problems must take special precautions in hot weather. Since the release of heat by the body is accomplished by a transfer of heat from the core to the peripheral blood vessels, anything that impedes this transfer can limit your ability to cope with heat. Atherosclerosis, smoking, hypertension, diabetes, and advanced age may all increase risks. If any of these characteristics pertain to you, see your physician before you launch your boat on a hot day. Heat stress can accumulate over several days. If you feel bad on a hot day, stop, go home, take a cold shower, eat lots of bananas or other potassium-rich fruits and drink lots of water.

Pollution

Pollution affects scullers in several ways. Air pollution can leave you choking and gasping after an interval workout. Water pollution caused by chemicals and other wastes can potentially cause cancer. Undoubtedly some poor sculler on some body of water has had to replace his equipment due to corrosion caused by high levels of acid or other nasty substances dumped upriver.

A couple of hard and fast rules should keep you protected from your fellow man's environmental depredations. If the air pollution levels are high enough to elicit a pollution advisory or warning from the local government, either go inside or sharply curtail your intensity of work. It seems high pollution levels are always accompanied by high humidity and high temperatures; the potential health problems associated with these conditions should convince you to scull another day with lungs and heart intact.

High air pollution levels can be especially harmful when the air contains too much carbon monoxide. High carbon monoxide levels can limit your body's ability to use oxygen, reducing your ability to perform aerobic and anaerobic work. Carbon monoxide hampers your blood's oxygen-carrying ability by binding to the hemoglobin in the red blood cells. With the hemoglobin effectively filled up, it cannot pick up oxygen in the lungs. This lack of oxygen can significantly impair your ability to perform. You can usually rid yourself of the carbon monoxide within a few hours; but if you are stuck in traffic in July while on your way to the river and your head is hanging out the car window, skip the workout and head home instead.

Unless you know for a fact that the water you row on has been purified, do not drink it. There are several areas where one can drink the water one sculls on, but you may get giardia poisoning (a really nasty gastrointestinal problem) from imbibing water from a seemingly pristine wilderness river just as you may contract some exotic disease from drinking the water in Baltimore's Middle River. Bring your own water instead, as the benefit (short-term relief of thirst) is not worth the potential cost (lost season due to serious illness).

Fog

If you can't see the other side of the river you can't go out. You may want to select some point about 300 yards from your launching spot and proclaim the visibility of said point to be the deciding factor in answering the "to row or not to row" question. Be especially careful if there are other folks on the river and do not hesitate to inform them of your presence. Fog distorts sound so someone may be a lot closer than they sound coming from a different direction. Lights seem to help others to locate you in fog but they get absorbed in the mist rather quickly, so sometimes you may not see someone until he is literally right on top of you.

Don't do high-intensity work in fog or low-light conditions; you're just inviting trouble. If you really have to get that workout in that day at that time, hop on an erg. Fog days are for technique rows at half and three-quarter pressure. Of course, you could always wait for the fog to burn off, which usually happens an hour or two after sunrise. Your insurer would undoubtedly appreciate your patience.

Lightning and Thunderstorms

Many areas of the country are subject to thunderstorms on hot summer afternoons. These storms come up suddenly and bring high winds, lightning, and sometimes torrential rain. If you are on the water and a storm blows up, head for home as fast as your little legs will take you.

If you are caught out, you may try lying down in the boat to reduce your chances of getting struck by lightning. However, since you're probably in more danger from high winds and the resulting waves, and because it is pretty tough to control your boat while you are flat on your back, try to get home instead.

If you do scull in the afternoon, listen to the weather report on your way to the river. You may be able to avoid a storm by sculling away from it, but they move around and another one might be right behind the first. Avoid the problem altogether by sculling in the morning.

INJURIES

Sculling is perhaps the most injury-free sport, second only to swimming. Injuries do occasionally occur. These injuries are often caused by too much work too soon, mechanical abnormalities or technical flaws. If you use some common sense and understand your limitations, you'll have a long and injury-free career. If you don't use good judgment, you may well end up with one of the maladies described below.

There are two types of injuries: cause-specific and post-exercise pain. Cause-specific injuries can be traced to a specific cause or causes; post-exercise pain is caused by localized overexertion.

Post-exercise Pain

Post-exercise pain is most frequently found in untrained and/or out-of-shape people who try to do too much. Ex-scullers are particularly susceptible to post-exercise pain because they try to do the workouts they did as young, conditioned athletes when they haven't picked up an oar in a long time. If you fit into this category, a special warning for you and an admonition to carefully consider your getting-back-into-shape plans.

The difficult thing about post-exercise pain is it varies widely in regard to severity, location of pain, and time until onset. There do seem to be several factors that predispose one toward post-exercise pain. A lack of local muscular endurance, a lack of strength in the exercising muscles, fatigue, poor psychological state, failure to adequately warm up or cool down, or some combination will increase your chances of experiencing post-exercise pain. If you feel physically terrible after sculling and you completed the workout even though you were exhausted and hadn't warmed up, now you know why.

Post-exercise pain is most commonly felt after a bout of severe exercise. Four major categories of post-exercise trauma are based on the timing of the onset of pain.

Acute Traumatic Pain

Acute traumatic pain occurs immediately after exercise. It is probably caused by the release of cellular materials into the spaces around the cells. These materials stimulate pain receptor nerves which tell your brain you are in pain. You can avoid or reduce the pain by using an active recovery that might include light rowing. In many cases the pain disappears even without an active recovery.

Acute Metabolic Pain

Acute metabolic pain also starts immediately after exercise and continues for up to 24 hours. This is the aching pain in the legs that's with you all the way home in the car. It is caused by large, excessive amounts of lactic acid and other metabolic by-products produced when you scull very hard. The funny thing about this type of pain is it generalizes throughout the body; the blood seems to transport the wastes from the exercising muscles throughout the body, so your arms hurt, your face hurts, everything hurts. Acute metabolic pain can be remedied by active cool-down and stretching exercises.

Chronic Structural Pain

Chronic structural pain shows up a day or two after exercise and can persist for several more days. If you are experiencing pain much beyond 48 hours and stretching does you no good, you are probably experiencing chronic structural pain. There are several different levels of chronic structural pain, all of which are caused by structural damage to the muscle fiber and connective tissue. The damage can range from the tear of a few muscle fibers to the complete tearing of an entire muscle and the membrane surrounding it. Your best approach to this problem is to avoid it in the first place by warming up correctly. Once you have chronic structural pain you should see a physician and describe clearly and completely your activities over the last several days before the onset of the pain. If at all possible, talk to a doc who knows something about sculling or sports medicine.

Chronic Neuromuscular Pain

Chronic neuromuscular pain presents symptoms similar to chronic structural pain. It appears 24 to 48 hours after exercise and persists. Chronic neuromuscular pain is directly caused by the nerves as opposed to the muscle fibers themselves. The indirect causes of this type of pain should be pretty familiar by now. They include bouncing stretching (ballistic stretching) and the performance of motions an athlete is not properly conditioned for.

All post-exercise pain can be alleviated, if not eliminated, by proper warm-up and cool-down activities and a gradual increase in the intensity and duration of exercise over several weeks or months. The most important part of the warm-up and cool-down for preventing post-exercise pain is the stretching routine.

Static stretching should be used as part of both the warm-up and cool-down. Static stretching is the gradual and controlled lengthening of a muscle as the associated joint is held in a fixed or locked position. The position should be held for at least ten seconds and preferably more. Static stretching affects the nerves innervating a muscle, allowing the muscle to relax and lengthen, and decreasing the chance that sudden stretching can damage the muscle fiber. Muscle contracts more forcefully when it is prestretched.

Cause-specific Pain

If you don't warm-up and cool down properly, some awful things can happen. The areas most vulnerable to injury among scullers are the hand, wrist, back, upper chest, and knee.

Hands.

The most common injury in sculling is the blister. Blisters arise when you first get on the water in the spring or any time you significantly increase your work on either the erg or the boat. You'll get blisters on the palm-side of the thumb and between the joints on the fingers.

If you are sculling every day, you cannot let the blisters heal themselves on their own schedule. If you do, you will find your hands are always sore and bleeding because the constant friction from sculling tears off the skin over the blisters and exposes the new skin underneath. The only way to prevent this is to drain the blister immediately after it blows up and keep it drained. This treatment plan will give you a callus much faster than if you wait for the blister to naturally heal itself.

To drain a blister, heat a sharp pin in a flame or dip it in alcohol to sterilize it. Puncture the blister at the very edge where it meets the skin, and squeeze the liquid out onto a tissue. If the liquid is clear, the blister is not infected. Keep the blister uncovered so it can dry out. If the liquid is milky or dark, the blister is infected. Soak the affected digit or area in alcohol. It doesn't feel very good but it usually kills the infection and dries up the wound.

Before you head down to the boat, check your hands to see if the blisters are healing up well. If the new skin is still soft, you may want to tape over the affected area so it doesn't get torn off during your next row. Try not to use regular white athletic tape because the adhesive tends to soften skin and can cause more blisters if it rolls up while you scull. Try one of the commercially-available athletic tapes that is not affected by water, only sticks to itself, and has a fairly open weave. Use a minimal amount of tape. Too much tape will reduce your feel for the handles and will probably come off as you scull, causing more blisters and making a mess out of your oar handles.

If your hands get really sore and tender, you may want to try soaking them in a very hot solution of soap and disinfectant, such as betadine. The solution should be hotter than you can stand. It's just about the right temperature if you can't keep your hands in the bowl for more than a few seconds at a time.

After blisters comes a callus, and if you don't keep your callus trimmed, you'll find new blisters forming under the callus. Every so often use a fingernail clipper to take the top layer of callus off. You don't want to have thick pads of callus: you just want enough to protect the contact areas of the hands from friction.

A relatively common problem, especially among athletes who have recently begun intense training, is sculler's thumb. A logical name as the problem is caused by sliding the palm down toward the bottom while trying to keep the thumb over the end of the grip. If you do this enough, you will get pain toward the back of the thumb spreading up the forearm. Treatment plans call for ice, massage, and perhaps an anti-inflammatory medicine to reduce the swelling. In severe cases ultrasound and even immobilization may be required.

Wrists.

Wrist pain can be caused by using the wrists too much when feathering. The solution is to eliminate the cause of the problem (poor technique) and perhaps strengthen the wrist muscles. You might find ice therapy helps to minimize any swelling and reduce the pain.

One particular type of wrist pain is sculler's wrist, described in medical terms as traumatic tenosynovitis of the wrist extensors (just in case a doctor ever tells you this is your problem).

Symptoms of this malady are pain, swelling, and tenderness along with a crackling sensation (known as crepitus to medical folks) when you move your wrist. What causes sculler's wrist is a sculling-induced enlargement of some of the muscles in the wrist. These enlarged muscles press on other muscles underneath them, causing pain and other symptoms.

Back.

Probably the most commonly injured anatomical area is the back. One advantage scullers have over sweep rowers is that the pulling action used in sculling is symmetrical as opposed to the twisting movement required by the sweep stroke. This twisting motion results in unequal loads on different parts of the back and often results in overdevelopment of one side of the back. Injuries may arise because of this situation; injuries that will not occur in scullers because the stress placed on the back is equally distributed on both sides.

Again, injuries should be distinguished from post-exercise pain. Sculling, especially hard interval training, puts a lot of stress on all parts of the body, so one should expect some pain and soreness after a hard workout. Women and new scullers are at especially high risk for back trouble because their legs are often quite strong relative to the upper body. This overdevelopment means the legs can generate more force than the back (and the rest of the upper body) can comfortably handle.

If you are just starting out in the sport, make it a point to include back-strengthening exercises in your training. Many of the injuries described below can be prevented, or their deleterious effects minimized, if the back's muscles and connective tissue are strong and flexible.

Sculling in very rough water can result in trauma. If your blades can't lock solidly into the water when you are sculling at full power, the resulting violent slippage of the blade, particularly if it is only one blade, puts a lot of strain on the back. Your back isn't prepared for the added stress.

The back's muscles, ligaments, joints, and discs are all subject to stress and injury. Muscular pain is often of the post-exercise variety and may be relieved with aspirin, massage, and gentle heat. If the pain persists for several days, you may have a flaw in your technique or a rigging problem that is contributing to, or the sole cause of, the discomfort.

One of the more common back problems is called scapulo-costal syndrome. This malady is often seen in people with a tendency to overreach when sculling. It is marked by a rounding of the shoulders as the sculler tries to extend out as far as possible. Mechanically this rounding of the shoulders protracts, or extends the shoulder blades (scapula) and stretches the attached muscles. If you are unfortunate enough to be afflicted with this, your first signal will be a pain starting between the shoulder blades and the spine. The pain may be a sharp point or a generalized ache and will radiate out from that area if you continue to scull. Generally, it feels worse when you get tired. The symptoms can be relieved by ice, massage, and perhaps medicine, but the cause of the injury must be eliminated.

Persistent pain lasting more than a couple of weeks may also be the result of friction between muscles sliding against each other. Although muscles normally slide freely, scar tissue covering minute tears in the fascia, or covering over the muscle, may cause the two muscles to "stick" to each other. If you have persistent pain in your back, consult a chiropractor, physical therapist, or osteopath.

Pain that's deep and aching is probably emanating from ligaments and not muscles. This is the kind of pain you experience after doing a long, steady-state piece, and it is caused by overstretching the connective tissue. Often the pain can be relieved by stretching. If your back hurts during a workout, try arching your back toward the bow and rolling your shoulders for a minute or two. It may not eliminate the pain but it can reduce it somewhat.

The spine is actually a continuous set of joints between each vertebra. The vertebrae themselves are held together with ligaments, which can be overstretched by a sudden, forceful movement. You will know when this happens; the pain is intense and sharp and it hurts to move in any direction.

There is not a whole lot you can do about this type of injury beyond resting, stretching, and limiting your movement. An anti-inflammatory medication such as aspirin may help to reduce the swelling around the injury. Do not try to jump back in the boat too soon, as you may well increase the damage. Instead, try some gentle stretching, stopping before the back hurts, and get back into sculling slowly. You may try some easy erg work before you get into the boat; if you experience any pain, you can stop right then. This is far better than sculling out a mile or two, feeling the pain come on, and sculling back as the pain and the damage increase. If you insist on sculling with this type of injury, you are increasing your chances of contracting osteoarthritis when you get older.

Disc problems are the most complex and potentially the most serious back injury. If you injure a disc, you may not feel the pain until a few hours after the row; even then your back may not hurt because the pain may feel as if it were in your rear end or legs. You may also have a sensation of pins and needles in your lower extremities. If this happens to you, do not try any of the therapies mentioned above, go see a doctor. Disc problems can be quite serious and you shouldn't scull until it has been checked out thoroughly. Depending on your own inclinations, you may want to see an orthopedic physician or a chiropractor.

Upper chest.

Chest pain was often diagnosed as a pulled intercostal muscle, but you may have a stress fracture of a rib or ribs if the pain lasts more than 10 days. The best way to determine if your problem is a stress fracture is to have a bone scan done by an orthopedist. If your diagnosis is a stress fracture, you should be able to begin training again within a couple of weeks and be back to full speed within six to eight weeks. If you continue to train through the pain, you could do a lot more damage to the bone, so don't be a macho idiot and ruin your season.

Your ribs may have fractured as a result of intense training, either on the water or in the weight room. Stress fractures usually show up two to four weeks after a significant increase in the intensity and/or volume of training, making it hard to diagnose the actual cause. To understand the cause of the problem, you have to remember that bone is living stuff that supports the body and provides attachment points for muscles. When you are pulling or lifting hard, the muscles actually deform the bones slightly, pulling them out of their natural shape. Over time, the bones actually grow stronger as a result of this training and can handle the increased load; but if you increase the load too soon or by too much, the bones don't have enough time to adapt. So, they fracture slightly.

Knees.

 Knee pain is one of the more unusual injuries among scullers. It can affect those individuals who are unfortunate enough to have a misalignment of the knee joint. The cause of most knee pain among scullers is centered on the patella, or knee cap. The patella slides in a groove in the femur, or thigh bone. If the patella repeatedly slides out of the proper groove, the friction of the rubbing of the patella against the femur can deteriorate the back of the patella. This condition, known as chondromalacia patellae, is more common among runners than scullers; so if you run a good bit, you may experience it as well.

The symptoms are swelling, pain, and tenderness of the joint, particularly around the patella. If you insist on exercising through the pain, you stand a pretty good chance of developing osteoarthritis and permanently damaging the cartilage around the joint. One of the scary things about chondromalacia patella is it leads to a deterioration of the vastus medialis muscle, the middle muscle in the quadriceps. One of the more successful solutions to this problem is to wear an elasticized brace around the knee, forcing the patella to slide in the correct groove. Don't try to diagnose this problem yourself; knee pain may be due to tendonitis or other causes exacerbated by the use of an elasticized brace.

You may be able to prevent the recurrence of knee pain by adjusting the angle of your foot stretchers. If your foot stretchers are forcing your patella to move in an inappropriate manner, no bracing or therapy is going to provide any lasting relief. You may want to try removing all the bolts attaching the shoes to the crossmember except for one in the middle. This will allow your foot to swivel around until it finds the best angle for itself. Occasionally rigging may actually cause knee pain.

Sculling is very safe and can provide a lifetime of great exercise and enjoyment if you use some common sense. If it hurts after a mile or so, stop. If it doesn't get any better, see a doctor. If it looks dangerous or unrowable, it is. If it is too hot or too cold, too windy or too dark, stay in bed or get an early start on the day's paperwork.

You can protect yourself from 90 percent of the bad things that may happen to you if you exercise good judgment before you exercise.

WOMEN AND SCULLING

Perhaps the biggest distinction between female and male scullers is the difference in relative upper body strength between novice women and novice men. The average woman tends to have less upper body strength than the average man. Women who have properly trained for a year or more are likely to have substantially increased their upper body strength. This additional strength is important not only because it makes them faster but also because it reduces the chance of injury and the severity of the injury if it does occur.

Pregnant women should be very careful about their heart rate during exercise. If you are pregnant, don't start sculling without seeing your physician first, and if you get pregnant, stop sculling until you can consult your doctor. In all likelihood the good doctor will okay aerobic training but rule out any intense work. You should keep your heart rate below your anaerobic threshold to make sure the baby gets enough oxygen.

If you don't get too big too soon, you may be able to scull well into the second trimester, although your stroke will probably shorten up a good bit. Your body will give you pretty strong hints when it is time to stop sculling: You won't be able to touch your footstretchers or row more than half slide. The boat will still be there after the baby is born and then you'll finally have a good name for it.

Lightweight women in particular have to watch their diet and menstrual cycle. The combination of hard training and efforts to make weight can sometimes lead to changes in the menstrual cycle and even temporary cessation of menstruation. Whenever your body fat percentage drops below 10 to 12 percent there is an increased risk of menstrual cycle irregularities, or amenorhea. If you are considering dieting, consult your physician and keep the doc informed about your condition.

KIDS AND SCULLING

There really are few problems associated with children sculling. Since most kids don't take up sculling until high school or junior high at the earliest, they are already physically able to withstand the rigors of an intelligently planned and well-executed training program. Although sculling may present its own set of risks, on the whole it compares favorably with more traditional sports such as football and hockey.

If your children are serious about sculling, they may begin weight training and other activities to improve their on-water performance. Strenuous weight training is potentially damaging to children's bones, as the ends of the bones are still growing and vulnerable to damage. Lifting moderate weights however should help them to achieve their goals and certainly should do no harm. If you are unsure, consult your physician.

Chapter Ten

Racing

lthough you may not be interested in racing when you start sculling, sooner or later the urge to test yourself, to compare yourself with your fellow scullers, will overtake you. By taking the time to understand your strengths and weaknesses, to identify realistic but aggressive goals, and to develop a strategy based on them before you begin racing, you'll find yourself well prepared and confident as you row to the starting line. If you just jump into races planning to row as hard and high as you can for as long as you can, you simply will not race to your potential. Invest the time before you begin racing each season and you will be much more likely to attain your goals.

Sculling races have their modern-day roots in the capitalistic motivations of watermen on the Thames River in England. According to most accounts, waterborne taxis would race to pick up passengers, with the fastest scullers rewarded with the most fares. Not surprisingly, these informal races tended to be fiercely aggressive affairs—the livelihood of the watermen and their families depended on their speed.

The daily competition of the watermen soon gave rise to more formal events. On August 1, 1716, the first recorded sculling race, Doggett's Coat and Badge, was held to determine who was the fastest sculler on the Thames. This race is still run today between London Bridge and Chelsea.

In the late 1800s and early 1900s professional sculling was one of the most popular sports in North America. Thousands of dollars were bet on races between the fastest scullers from the United States and Canada. Newspapers actually had reporters, including such budding authors as Bret Harte, covering the sport full-time to keep an anxious and enthusiastic public up to date on the workouts and health of top scullers.

Sculling drifted into relative obscurity as the 1900s progressed, in part due to a series of scandals involving scullers throwing races for the benefit of certain bettors. Although professional sculling has gone the way of the fixed seat, racing itself has really changed very little since the race for Doggett's Coat and Badge. Distances have varied, additional events have been added for crews of two or more, and technique, equipment, and conditioning have evolved, but the key is still crossing the finish line before anyone else.

There are three basic races: head races, which cover from two-and-a-half to four miles; sprint races, which are either 1000 or 2000 meters, and open-water racing, which may be any distance up to sixty miles. There are numerous variations on these three types of races. Some large regattas also have a "dash" event covering 500 meters or a quarter-mile, and some fall regattas are only 1500 meters. The basic concepts of strategy, focus, preparation, and tactics discussed below can apply to any type of race but especially head races and sprint races.

PERSONAL ASSESSMENT

When you first start racing you have no real frame of reference to set goals or assess your performance. Your friends and other acquaintances in the sculling world can tell you which races are likely to be more competitive, what conditions you are likely to encounter at different courses, and which scullers have been successful in the past. Hearing about it and experiencing it yourself are two very different things. You will increase your chances for success if you have set goals, done your training, planned effectively, and concentrated. There are no shortcuts.

If you're new at this sport, haven't raced before, and want to start racing, make sure you are as prepared as you can be before you row to the starting line.

First, analyze your desire to race. Are you really enthusiastic about sculling in a race? Do you want to race to see how you are progressing or because your fellow scullers think it would be a good idea? Remember, this is sculling, not some game. No one else will come on to the field to give you a breather or call a time out to give you a chance to regroup. You will succeed, or not, because you want to.

Second, assuming you do really want to race, well before the racing season begins you should objectively review the physiological and technical foundation you are building. How good is your technique? Do you have sufficient water time for a race to serve as a valid indicator of your current ability and future potential? Are you sure you've done the right type and amount of work necessary to be physiologically prepared for racing?

SEASONAL PLANS

Your plan for the season includes such things as the races you want to compete in, races you want to peak for, general training guidelines, and periodic evaluation sessions. Think of your season as a planned campaign with specific, planned milestones.

If you are anticipating your first season, the most important thing you can do is to set goals based on what you want to accomplish during that season. Too many scullers go into a season with no plan, no idea of what they want to achieve, and no clue as to how to realize their goals. At the end of the season they do not know if the season was good, bad, or indifferent because they had no goals to serve as a reference point. Moreover, they do not know what to do to improve their performance for next year.

At the beginning of the season, or better yet some months before when you actually start training, set goals for the upcoming season and for each race during the season. Sure, it may be months before the season's opening race, but you have to give yourself a goal to think about as you work through the winter months, something to give those mornings in the weight room some tangible purpose.

Your goals for the season might be as modest as finishing each race or as ambitious as winning the Olympic single trials. The season's goals will determine how you approach each race and what your goals are for that race. Write down the goals in your logbook and review them periodically. If necessary, revise them based on your progress in training, injuries, or schedule conflicts, but do not do so lightly. If you frequently change your goals, they lose their value as a reference point and motivator.

When developing your goals, be as specific as possible and be aggressive yet realistic. Setting a vague goal such as "I want to enjoy my sculling more" or "I want to be faster" isn't going to help. Identify exactly what you want to accomplish, such as, "I want to row 2000 meters in calm conditions under 7:20 by the National Championships." Specific goals enable you to go back to your logbook and see where you made mistakes and where you performed well. This learning process teaches valuable lessons that will form the basis for future improvement.

You will be successful if you set goals that are just a little bit above you so you can strive to attain them. You will derive enormous satisfaction when you do. Setting goals too low won't force you to do your best. Conversely, setting unachievably high goals may frustrate and depress you. Either way, you'll lose the joy of training. More than likely your goals will revolve around one race or a couple of races for which you want to peak. If so, your training schedule and the entire season will be structured around preparing for the key event. There will undoubtedly be other races, physiological evaluation sessions, and other non-sculling events you will want to factor into your seasonal plan. When planning your schedule, remember you can peak perhaps twice a year. If you plan very well and are blessed by the sculling gods, you may be able to peak a third time as well.

As part of the seasonal plan, make decisions on which races you will enter based on your ability and confidence level. Especially when you are just getting into the sport, the more racing you do, the better. Don't worry about coming in barely ahead of the boats in the race after yours. You are learning how to race. Each person responds differently to the stresses of racing; the more racing you do, the more you will know about your own reaction to these stresses, and the smarter you will become.

RACE STRATEGY

Once you've established your seasonal plan you can work on your basic race strategy. This strategy is the one you will develop and refine throughout the training and competitive parts of the season. It is the basic strategy you will use in all your races. Do not hurry through this process. You are devoting serious amounts of time and giving up trips to the beach, David Letterman, and promotions to positions in arid climates because you want to go fast. Don't shortchange yourself by ignoring the most important part of your preparation.

A race strategy is an evolving thing. It should take into account your technical and physiological strengths and weaknesses, past experience, and psychological characteristics. For example, if it is early in the season and you haven't worked on your closing sprint yet, your race plan might call for you to start pushing the pace at the halfway mark. As the season progresses, you can gradually incorporate a sprint in your race strategy. The key is to understand what gives you the best chance of success and design your strategy accordingly.

There are three components involved in developing race strategy. These components include your unique physiological, mental, and technical characteristics, the structure or framework upon which a plan is built (your race strategy), and the circumstances unique to each race.

Before you develop a race strategy, consider the nature of sculling races. Unlike other sports, sculling races usually begin with the athlete sprinting away from the starting line. The sculler then settles into a more modest pace until the finish approaches, whereupon the sprinting begins again. This is about as dumb as you can get.

By sprinting at the beginning of the race you build up a sizeable oxygen debt that you then have to carry the length of the course. Physiologically, this is crazy. But even though this strategy flies in the face of logic and science and hurts a lot as well, many scullers still use it, even in head races. Make sure you select a strategy that is best for you because it uses your strengths, hides your flaws, and emphasizes your talents. Don't pick a strategy because everyone else uses it.

PHYSIOLOGICAL, TECHNICAL, AND MENTAL CHARACTERISTICS

One of the more important influences on your sculling career is your muscle cell type. The only way to significantly influence this key factor is to choose your parents carefully; your second-best bet is to determine what your characteristics are and build a strategy from there. If you were sleeping through that part of the book, go back and reread it. These concepts are crucial to designing an intelligent, effective race plan.

Although there are a lot of other physiological factors involved in determining the most scientifically appropriate race strategy, (such as anaerobic threshold, oxygen uptake, and strength characteristics), they are all closely related to muscle-fiber composition. Scullers with predominantly fast-twitch muscle fiber are able to generate a lot of power and get off the line quickly, but incur an oxygen debt when they take advantage of this ability. Conversely, slow-twitch scullers do not build up lactic acid as quickly but are poor sprinters. Once you have determined your predominant muscle-fiber type, you have an important tool upon which to build a race strategy.

If you are a fast-twitch person, there are two basic strategies to follow. Taking up a sport more suitable to your physiology was an option, but you are in too deep now to go back to gymnastics or ice dancing. Understand that while you can generate a lot of power which should translate into speed, you can only do this for a limited time. Your options are either to blast out at the start, build an insurmountable lead, and hope you run out of race course before you blow up. Or, you can go out easily, carefully husbanding your burst of power until the sprint. If you can maintain contact with the pack, you will be in a good position to power right through them. Just be aware that's a big "if."

If you have been blessed with an abundant supply of slow-twitch cells, your options, although limited, are more attractive. Your best bet physiologically is to push the pace in the middle 1000 meters of the race, taking advantage of your ability to generate more power over a longer period than your fast-twitch competitors. This strategy will force the late sprinters to go harder than they want in the middle of the race, leaving their energy sources severely depleted just when they want to start their sprint. Conversely, the blast-off-the-line scullers will be pushed all the way down the course, all the while realizing they have little fuel in the tank with which to respond to your continuous pressure. Jim Wells of Philadelphia's University Barge Club refers to the moment of truth for these people as third stage separation: if they aren't ahead when they run out of fuel, their competitors will get to watch the fast starters fade over the horizon.

In addition to the purely scientific factors such as cell type, there are a number of other factors that must be considered in developing your basic race strategy. Psychological traits are undoubtedly the most important of these factors; some people might contend they are even more important. Some scullers don't like to set the pace, others want to hide in the pack until the final 500 meters, while still others need to believe they are the underdog to reduce the pressure (self-induced) on them to perform well.

For example, perhaps you are racing a 2000-meter distance, have terrific oxygen uptake, predominantly slow-twitch muscle fiber, and can't tolerate the pressure of rowing from behind. Although logic dictates a race plan that calls for you to row through your competition in the middle 1000, you will not be successful if you adopt this strategy. Instead, focus on developing a great start, learn to row at a high rating, and race a lot. A technically sound start should minimize the early lead of your blast-off-the-line competitors while raising your confidence level. As you get more experience racing and your confidence grows, you will be more poised in the heat of battle, and more likely to learn to row through people.

BASIC RACE STRATEGIES

There are four basic race strategies from which to choose: offensive, defensive, final sprint, and even splits. Most scullers find one they like and stick with it, although they may modify their strategy for a particular race.

Offensive Tactics

Offensive tactics are best suited to a sculler who is aggressive and possesses a good start. The plan involves a long starting sprint of perhaps 40 strokes that builds a substantial lead. The sculler then settles into a race pace and watches as the other scullers make their moves, prepared to counter any significant threats with 10 or 20 strokes at a slightly higher pressure or rating. The sculler using this strategy gains confidence if the plan works, because he is in control of the race. However, if someone else has the same strategy, you run the risk of killing each other off early in the race as you both fight for the lead. Another risk is you may blow up; the early sprint can build up an oxygen debt that you cannot carry for the rest of the race. Finally, the plan may just not work: you may not be able to take any lead at all.

Defensive Tactics

Defensive tactics are great for the slow but steady sculler who can't start or sprint well. In this case, put everything into the middle 1000 meters, especially from 800 to 1500 meters. This constant pressure will eat into the offensive sculler's lead, and his power tens should eventually lose their effectiveness. At that point you simply row through him on the way to the awards dock.

Final Sprint

Scullers favoring the final sprint always rattle their opponents because one never knows how much the sprinter has left.

Psychologically these people are tough to row against, because if they are anywhere within striking distance, the other scullers will worry about what the sprinter is doing instead of concentrating on their own sculling. The race plan is pretty simple: row the first 1500 meters hard enough to maintain contact with the leaders then start cranking it up with 500 meters to go.

Scullers using this strategy almost never row up to their potential because they have to save their energy for the end of the race. That being said, a recent trials for the U.S. men's light single were won by Kevin Bedell with a great final sprint. Still, this is a great strategy for the first part of the season when you may not yet know what the best pace is for you. Moreover, chances are the other scullers haven't even begun to think about working on a sprint, so you can catch them by surprise.

Even Splits

The most intelligent, logical, and successful strategy is also the hardest one to execute. If you can row even times for each quarter of the race, you will go as fast as you can. You may not win, but you will row your best possible time. The problem with this strategy is it operates in a vacuum; it assumes that the most important factor in winning a race is a sculler's speed over the distance. It isn't.

If you know you are the fastest sculler (or close to it) in a race, you will succeed rowing even splits. This is because even splits are the most physiologically efficient strategy: You know you are the fastest sculler in the race and no tactical move by another sculler will shake your faith. But what if you're not the fastest sculler? You can most definitely increase your chances of success by adopting one of the other race strategies. The reason is psychology. You may rattle your competitors, even the faster, even-splits scullers, by racing smart. They may start to think you are training harder or maybe their faith in their speed, desire, and strategy is not unshakeable. If you do something out of character, perhaps hanging back at the start and putting on a big effort at the halfway mark, other scullers may waste valuable time trying to figure out what the heck you are up to.

The even-splits strategy is still the best one. Technically, it makes a lot of sense. According to the famous German coach Karl Adam, even pacing gives you the most speed for the amount of effort you produce because of the law of diminishing returns: the faster you go the more resistance the boat encounters. Moreover, you produce high levels of lactic acid for a small increase in speed.

Pertti Karpinen provides a good example of the effectiveness of the even-splits strategy. Karpinnen, a three-time Olympic gold medalist in the single, is famous for rowing through the pack in the last part of the race. He is able to do this because he knows the pace he can maintain for 2000 meters and allocates his energy stores evenly over the course of the race.

Karpinnen used the traditional strategy (starting sprint, settle, sprint at the end) in the 1976 Olympic heats. His split times for each 500 meters of the race were 1:40, 1:50, 1:54, 1:49; just good enough for fourth place. The next race was the repechage, or second chance, for scullers who did not win the heats to try and qualify for the semis. Karpinnen modified his strategy somewhat, rowing 1:41, 1:48, 1:50, 1:48. This effort was sufficient to move him into the semifinals, where, using the same strategy, he qualified for the finals by placing third.

The finals were to be the coronation of Peter-Michael Kolbe. Kolbe was the odds-on gold medal favorite. Karpinnen had never beaten Kolbe before, but he had never used the even-splits strategy either. The three preliminary races were learning experiences; Karpinnen could now closely estimate the fastest pace he could maintain over the entire 2000 meters, and he knew his competitors' strategies as well as their best times so far.

In the first 500 meters of the final, Karpinnen was a distant last. His time of 1:53 put him over three lengths in back of Kolbe, who had rowed a 1:47. In the second 500 meters Karpinnen continued to fall back. Again rowing a 1:53, Karpinnen lost an additional three seconds to Kolbe. This put him five lengths out of first—a virtual time zone—with 1000 meters to go.

Even though he sagged a little, Karpinnen gained two lengths on Kolbe in the third 500, rowing a 1:54.5. Kolbe was feeling the effort that had gained him the lead; his third 500 split was 1:59. Although Kolbe sprinted in the last 500, dropping his split down to 1:56, it was a futile effort. Karpinnen, sensing victory, rowed a 1:49 and won the gold handily.

Now for the reality check. The even-splits strategy sounds like a great idea. All you have to do is figure out how fast you can go for 2000 meters, hit your splits, and you will go as fast as you can, hopefully winning the race. The reality is somewhat more complicated. Go back and look at Karpinnen's race again. He was down nine seconds, or five lengths, with 1000 meters to go. Psychologically, it's very tough to race all out, to reach deep within yourself for your best effort when you cannot see the leader without swiveling your head completely around. And, if you can catch a glimpse, you may be appalled by the distance you have to make up. This is why unshakeable faith is vital to the success of the even-splits strategy and why racing smart can mean selecting other strategies.

Qualifying Heats

When you get fast, there is one other race plan you will use, albeit rarely. For a couple of very good reasons, you will race differently in qualifying heats than you will in the final. First, it makes no sense to show your competition your entire hand. As with poker, they will have to pay to see it. Second, you should expend enough energy to absolutely assure your advancement to the next race—be it the semifinals or finals—and no more. Once you are positive you are in the final, it is wasteful to use up energy stores you will need later. But be positive you are in before you start an energy conservation program. It is no fun driving home down the interstate chanting "I am an idiot" for several hours. I know, I've done it.

No matter what, always race the first 1000 meters hard. Then, if you are definitely in the final at that point, slow the slide, perhaps take a little off the stroke, and concentrate on sculling well. As you get closer to the finish line, you may want to decrease the pressure a little as long as you are still confident of your position. Keep your eyes open and watch every lane, especially the lanes farthest from you.

Conversely, if you are behind, never give up. Dig in and keep going. You may catch someone napping; if you don't and lose anyway, you can take pride in your effort.

Some scullers race for specific finishing positions in heats or semis. This strategy may make some sense if you want to avoid coming up against the favorite in the semis or if you believe a certain lane has an advantage over the others. It can also get awfully complicated and divert your attention from the more important things, such as sculling well. Just make sure you get into the finals.

ADAPTING TO CIRCUMSTANCES

Once you have a basic strategy set in your mind, you can start to develop a more detailed race plan, one adapted to the upcoming race. The details of this plan will vary from race to race depending on both internal and external factors. External factors include the conditions on the course, importance of the race, and the opponents you see on the starting line. It is important to consider your opponents' quality, probable race plans, strengths and weaknesses, and past history. If you do your homework, you won't be lulled into a sense of security when a fast sculler hangs back at the start. Since you know he is fast, you should suspect he has adopted an even-splits strategy. Also, you will remain calm if a fly-and-die sculler bolts past you in the first ten strokes. You know you'll overtake him about ten strokes after his oxygen debt really kicks in.

Internal factors to consider include the amount of sleep you got the night before, your level of conditioning, the equipment you will be using, your relative success previously on this particular race course, and your individual physiological and psychological attributes.

These factors all contribute to the way you decide to row a particular race on a particular day. Rarely will you completely change your race plan, but you may decide to row a stroke or two higher in a tailwind or shorten your starting sprint if the course is against the current and into a headwind. Be aware of changing conditions, adapt to them, and you will come closer to rowing up to your potential.

SPRINT RACING

Two thousand meters, or approximately a mile and three-sixteenths, is the standard distance for the summer racing season. Races are usually decided during one of four key points during those 2000 meters: the start, settle, third 500, and the final sprint. No matter what your basic race strategy, there is a right way to row each of these segments.

Before the Race

Before the race, have all the little details covered. Make sure your entry was accepted and confirm the starting time well in advance. If the race is out of town make up a checklist of everything you need to bring, including oars, riggers, seat, footstretchers, strokemeter, wiring harness, water bottle, tool kit, race numbers, slings, road map, directions to the regatta site, and anything else you deem essential for the event.

Get as much information before the race as possible. Find out exactly what time your event is, what lane you are in, and who the competition is. If there are heats for the final, find out how many advance to the final, how lanes are selected for the final, and what is the planned starting time. It's also a good idea to find out what the events preceding yours are so you will know if they are running late. If you have to check in at regatta headquarters and/or weigh in, ask what time they will be open. If you haven't been to this particular course before, find someone who has and learn where to park, what the traffic pattern on the water is, and where you can find drinking water and bathrooms.

Before you launch for the race, sit down in a quiet spot (the car is a good bet if you are away from home) and mentally rehearse the race one more time. If you've been using visualization techniques, you are well prepared for this rehearsal. Even if you haven't been practicing visualization, row the entire race in your mind. When you lose your concentration, bring your mind back to the race and continue visualizing each stroke. This mental warm-up can greatly improve your focus on the water; don't skip it. You have spent too much time preparing for this to get sloppy now.

The Warm-up

Finish whatever warm-up you use on land so you are ready to launch about 30 minutes before your race. If you are really jumpy, extend your land warm-up a little more. You may want to launch earlier if you have a long row to the start or a long warm-up. As you row away from the dock you may feel tired or weak, a natural reaction as adrenaline starts to flow. Don't use this as an excuse to back away from the warm-up; it is very important that you stick to your routine. Try to plan your warm-up so you are on the stakeboats just after finishing, when you are still breathing a little fast, and the sweat is flowing. Since many races are delayed, you will be much better off if you are a little warm when you pull up to the stakeboats than if you are already starting to cool down.

If you are not warmed up when you get to the stakeboat, you may want to risk jumping the start to get in a few more power strokes. Be forewarned, officials may be furious with this. If you are caught, you will have to be very careful not to jump the next start, since you'll be disqualified. On occasion you may get away with the jump and find yourself in the lead off the line. If you are so fortunate, don't be so surprised at your good luck that you squander your windfall. Remember that your fellow scullers will not be pleased with your antics and you will undoubtedly hear about it after the race.

The Start

Things happen too fast to think at the start, so make sure you have done all the preparing you can before race day. Several minutes before your event, the starter will notify all boats in the starting line area that the race will start at a specified time. The starter will call you and your competitors to the line and give you starting instructions. Normally these instructions include warnings on jumped starts, allowances for equipment breakage, and a review of the starting commands. The job of the aligner, who is right on the starting line, is to ensure that all the bows are right on the starting line. When the aligner is satisfied, the starter is notified.

Upon receiving notification from the aligner, the starting official will poll all the scullers, who acknowledge they have a course by nodding their heads. Since you were in the starting area for the start of the previous race, you have already heard the starter give the commands to begin a race. You can use this information to anticipate a start, but be prepared to get caught if you anticipate a little too much.

The official rule regarding starts is there can be movement in the boat but the boat cannot move. In other words, you can start sliding your seat toward the bow, but the boat cannot begin to move forward. Officials will usually call back races when scullers blatantly jump the start, although if the regatta is well behind schedule or the race is a heat, they are less likely to call you back for a restart. If you plan on anticipating the start, be prepared to take your chances; if you are caught, you will be charged with a false start. One more and you are disqualified, so be careful the next time.

The command has been given, the waiting is over. The start of the race is crucial; you must set the tone for the rest of the race by rowing a relaxed, powerful, smooth stroke. During the first few strokes make sure you are pressing your feet into the stretchers and drawing the oars in level. Your hands are high, keeping the blades buried; you want the boat to set up well to ensure the next stroke is effective. Sit up straight, breathe, and focus on sculling well. Do not look out of the boat; relative positions don't make any difference yet.

When you have lengthened out for the high strokes, focus on relaxing during the recovery. The number of high strokes you do before the settle is determined by your race plan and can vary from as few as 10 to as many as 40. Whatever number you select, make sure they are good ones. Too many scullers frantically slash at the water in the first 500 meters in an effort to get away fast. All this accomplishes is to incur a high oxygen debt and make the rest of the race easy on their competitors.

Don't be alarmed if you feel terrible during the start and for much of the first 500 meters. If you have cooled off somewhat while waiting for the start, your body will have to rely completely on anaerobic energy sources for the first minute of the race. Until your aerobic energy system kicks in you will be building up an oxygen debt and feeling the effects of it. Take it ten strokes at a time and you will feel a lot better by the second 500.

The Settle

The settle, the transition from the high stroking of the start to a cadence you'll use for the rest of the race, is the single most important part of the race. Done well, it results in little loss of speed as the higher stroke is exchanged for a lower, more

efficient rating. The settle gives you a chance to relax, get into a rhythm, and perhaps become aware of your position in the standings. After you settle look over your shoulder to check your course. Use your peripheral vision as much as possible and do not dwell on your relative position.

There are a couple of schools of thought on the most effective way to settle. Some scullers and coaches like to settle gradually, over several strokes. The natural tendency when gradually settling is to back off on the pressure ever so slightly to bring the rating down. Instead of risking this decrease in power, settle in one stroke.

The one-stroke settle is very simple, making it harder to screw up. For the last several strokes of the start focus on the proper settle technique, reminding yourself to take it down on the slide while still pressing the feet into the stretchers and drawing in firmly with the arms and back. When the settle stroke arrives, the only change is that the slide slows down; the hands come out just as fast, the legs drive just as hard, and the bladework is identical. Also, make a conscious effort to relax after the settle and focus on your sculling, not on the competition.

The normal reaction after the stress and excitement of the start is to let down at the first opportunity. It focuses the mind to take a very hard ten strokes several strokes into the settle. This serves two purposes: to minimize any advantage a competitor may gain by prolonging his start and to set the tone for the race.

Second 500

If you have not found your groove yet, or you feel tight in your forearms or somewhere else, use the second 500 to establish a relaxed stroke. This is the last chance for you to settle down, at least for this race.

You are now in the body of the race. Traditionally, little happens during the second 500. Whether this is because the sprinters are trying to catch their breath and the endurance scullers haven't started to take advantage of their physiology yet is unknown, but scullers rarely look back and identify this part as a critical stage in the race. You may try a power ten at this point to test the mettle of the competition, to see if they respond. A better idea might be to save this energy for when you will really need it, the third 500.

Third 500

Now you are starting to feel really poorly. If you were home lying in bed and had similar symptoms, you would be dialing 911. On the other hand, if you don't feel terrible around the halfway point, you haven't been pulling hard enough. Of the races not determined during the first minute, the vast majority are won and lost in the third 500. Why? Because this is the point where most scullers, prompted by the physical distress they are experiencing, decide to either go all out or pack it in. The effects of a diminished effort, even for a few strokes, will slow you down and give heart to your competitors.

Many scullers make a tactical move several strokes into the third 500. Because this part of the race is so crucial, whether or not your strategy calls for a move in the third 500, make a conscious effort to refocus your mind on the task at hand. Concentrate on sculling well and hanging on the oars all the way through the stroke. By focusing on your own performance and the finer points of technique, you are less likely to be affected by the physical distress you are experiencing or by any tactical moves others may be making.

If you plan on making a major effort at this point, make it a good one. Should your effort fall short of breaking contact with the field, they will be heartened by their performance and will come after you with blood in their eyes. Scullers tend to let up a little after a major move; focus on continuing to pull away after 10 or 20 hard strokes are completed. If you fail to take advantage of the lead gained by increasing your oxygen debt to almost maximal levels, your competitors will sense your weakness and take advantage of your distress.

There is another way to survive the dead zone of the third 500 and that awful feeling that comes when you realize you have just as far to go as you have already come and there is no way you will make it: lying. There are many different lies you can tell yourself, but the most effective is something involving a promise to yourself that you will never pick up an oar again if you somehow survive the next three or four minutes. When that time frame seems too long, the other survival method is employed: tell yourself you will stop rowing in ten strokes, but you will concentrate on getting the hands out smoothly and fast for those next ten strokes. When surviving ten is beyond comprehension, try five, then three. By the time you get to two more strokes you should be over the finish line. If not, you need to train more.

Last 500

At some point in the last 500 meters you will be faced with the decision whether or not to sprint and, if the answer is yes, when to start your sprint. The easy answer is you sprint only if you have to and begin the sprint at the point where you will be able to increase your speed and maintain it until just after the finish line, where you will collapse.

The homework really pays off here. If you know who in the race can sprint and who can't, you should be able to figure out the best time to start picking up the pace.

If you are in the lead and not threatened, don't bother to sprint as it will only increase your chances of making a mistake. Moreover, don't show something to the competition unless they force you to. If you do have to sprint, there are two basic techniques to choose: you can raise the rating or you can pull harder.

Many scullers actually go slower when they raise the rating for a sprint because they rush the slide, shorten up, and basically forget all about technique. Of all times to abandon good sculling (and there never is one), this is not it. Before the sprint actually begins, force yourself to relax and focus on the technical changes you will have to make to sprint effectively. Then, at the appointed time, sit up straighter and concentrate on getting the hands out fast. Don't worry about rowing long strokes; you aren't interested in looking good in the sprint, you want to get the most out of each stroke. That means using the legs. If you have been getting in your work, the legs should get you through the last few strokes.

Most scullers sprint by going up two strokes at the beginning of the sprint and again with 20 or so to go; you will learn what works for you through experience. Try raising the rating two strokes at the beginning of the sprint. If you think you can, try going up another stroke or two 20 strokes from the finish. Other scullers like to raise the rating once every five strokes. The rate doesn't actually increase that often. If it did, you'd find yourself rowing 40 well before the finish line made its appearance. The up-one-in-five strategy forces you to think about sitting up straight and helps you deal with this most painful part of the 2000 meters.

Pulling harder is the other method of sprinting. It is as simple in concept as it sounds, although it can be somewhat more difficult in execution. You should have little left in the tank when you get to the last 30 strokes, but there will be enough there to get you to the finish line. Again, focus on sculling well, hanging on the oars, and getting the hands out quickly and smoothly. Even though you aren't trying to raise the rating, sit up straighter. This shortens the stroke, making it more effective. It also prevents the common technical error of laying back too much in an effort to row longer and harder.

Finally, paddle once you are over the line. If you win by a tenth of a second or get beaten by 500 meters, don't stop sculling and do not fall apart after you cross the line. Keep your competitors guessing; if they see you scull away from the finish, they won't know how much the effort took out of you.

When you can speak without gasping, congratulate all the other scullers on a well-rowed race and wish them luck in their next event. Never, never exult when you win, at least not in public. Be proud, but respect the efforts of your fellow scullers. They alone can fully appreciate your achievement. That appreciation, born of shared experience and sacrifice, is what makes sculling the great sport it is.

HEAD RACING

Head races are races against the clock, with boats starting every ten seconds or so. Although not considered part of the regular racing season, head racing has become very popular. One of the largest regattas in the world is the Head of the Charles, a two-and-three-quarters–mile race over the serpentine Charles River in Boston. It is always oversubscribed. Only the fastest boats (those finishing within 5 percent of the winning time) get guaranteed entries the following year.

Head races are also a valuable training tool, enhancing your aerobic base after a summer spent sprinting over 2000 or 1000 meter courses. Since they are two-and-a-half times longer than the 2000 meter distance, head races force you to pay careful attention to technique. If you are checking the boat or have a sloppy release, you will have plenty of time to notice the negative effects of your technical imperfections.

With all the passing, steering, tactics, and sometimes wildly differing ability levels in the same event, head races can be a lot of fun. For the sculler who just can't muster the speed to win a sprint race, head races offer a chance to tortoise the sprint hares who have been creaming you all summer.

Racing a head race depends in large part on the course and the conditions. As most head races are in the fall, the conditions can range from hot and windy to sleet and freezing rain. Your starting position also has a big impact on your race; a position well back in the field means you will have to contend with a lot of wakes from boats starting before you. On the other hand, races where you pass no one and no one passes you can be pretty boring.

As always you are far better off racing smart in a head race than just pulling hard. Know the course, steer often and well, and be aware of what is going on around you. If your faster competitors think only about pulling hard, you will surprise a lot of people.

The start of a head race can be very confusing. Lots of boats from your event and the events before and after yours are milling about, some coming very close to colliding as crews try to get in a last hard ten before the start. It is a good idea to memorize the two events immediately before yours so you know when to start your warm-up and when to approach the line.

When your race is called, approach the starting line slowly, finding the boats starting before you. Fall into place immediately behind the boat before you and stick close to its stern. Don't start too far back, as you will want to try and pass as quickly as possible to get the smooth water.

When you are within ten strokes of the start, check on your course and crank it up to full power. When you cross the line you should be rowing at full power at your race pace. Do not try to row 10 or 20 high strokes at the start, as the oxygen debt will kill you in a head race. Set a pace you can maintain for the entire distance (with some difficulty), relax, and scull well.

Keep a close eye on your course during the race. You are better off rowing three miles pretty fast than three-and-a-half miles really fast; take the time to go over the course ahead of time and identify key points such as turns, buoys, bridges, and other potential navigational hazards. Look over your shoulder often during the race. Some scullers tape a map of the course to their stern for reference; maps confuse me, but it may work for you.

Passing another boat is relatively simple on a straightaway, but can be very frustrating on a curve. You have the right of way when you put your bow alongside (inside the turn) the boat you are overtaking. That being said, few scullers will give way easily when you are passing them. Be prepared to fight your way through, but don't waste mental energy worrying about an unsportsmanlike sculler's behavior. Try not to hit anything much bigger than you, and keep your mind focused on your sculling and not on the beer-soaked crowds loudly ignoring your efforts.

Other than that, there isn't much to racing a head race.

Chapter Eleven

Team Boats

o some folks, team boats, defined as those with two or more scullers, are the antithesis of sculling. No more lone athlete proving his mettle against the elements, competitors, and the clock. No solitary test of one's will and fortitude, no sense of satisfaction like the feeling one gets from a well-rowed piece.

True, but team boats have their own set of unique challenges and rewards that you don't find in a single. In a single you don't have someone else to share a victory or commiserate with over. And a single definitely doesn't teach you how to work closely with others to achieve a common goal. However, the biggest benefit of the team boat is the race is a lot shorter. If you are used to rowing a single, you'll be amazed at how fast you cover the course in a team boat.

What may also amaze you is the hassle team sculling can become if not approached intelligently. You will have to find one—or more—scullers you feel comfortable rowing with, set a mutually convenient time to practice (always 5:45 a.m.), agree on a workout plan, find a boat and rig it, and constructively criticize each other's style. Chances are, the logistical difficulties will be outweighed by the personality conflicts. Be patient and mature about the situation, and you'll be rewarded with a cohesive crew and fast times.

TEAM SCULLING

Some folks scull in team boats because they don't have access to a single shell. For early or late season sculling, a team boat is quite a bit safer than a single. It is more stable and less likely to flip, a key consideration when the water temperature heads below 10°C.

Team boats also help you refine parts of your technique. Since a team boat is much faster than a single, you have to speed up your catch and release to match the speed of the boat. Since the oars go through the water more quickly in a team boat, your leg drive will also speed up to match the boat's speed. The quickness you learn rowing in a team boat will help you move a single that much more efficiently.

If you plan on racing, you'll have a lot more opportunities if you can race events other than the single. It is not unusual for scullers to race the single, jump in a double for another race, and finish the day off by doing another 2000 meters in a quad. Some folks are of the opinion that they have trained too hard to race only one event, so they row several events to get the best return on their training investment.

Finally, in some ways it's easier to scull in a team boat than in a single. If you're not quite at the point where you are moving the single well, you may find racing a double is a bit more rewarding.

The Boats

The most common sculling boats are double sculls (doubles) and quadruple sculls (quads). Octuple sculls have experienced a resurgence in the past few years but are still pretty unusual.

Triple sculls were popular around the turn of the century but have now disappeared from the scene, although you may still come across one on the upper rack in a boathouse.

The Crew

In team sculling it is more important to row together than to row well. Technique is all-important in sculling but in this case individual technical perfection takes a back seat to timing and consistent bladework. Two scullers may individually scull very well, yet be dead slow in a double. Conversely, two mediocre scullers who are cannon fodder in singles may mesh well in a double and do pretty well.

It is up to the bowman to adapt to the stroke's style. He may have to rush his slide, slow down his hands, or otherwise alter the technique he spent so many hours perfecting in order to make the boat go fast. In cases such as these, keep in mind the object is to move the boat; races are not awarded to those garnering the most style points from the judges. Of course, it is also the bowman's prerogative, in fact his job, to help the stroke correct technical flaws, but don't try to work on hand speed in the middle 1000 meters of a race.

Before your maiden voyage you'll have to decide who is responsible for steering. The choices are usually limited to the bowman or the stroke, although in a quad in some rare instances two or three may assume the responsibility (or, more likely, have it thrust upon him).

Leaving aside the crucial question of who in the boat has the best natural steering ability, there are situations where it is more appropriate for the occupant of one seat or another to assume the steering responsibilities. If you will be racing on a buoyed course, the stroke has the best vantage point since he has an unobstructed view of the lane markers off the stern. All he has to do is keep the stern centered on the appropriate lane marker.

If your sculling will be on a winding body of water or you'll be competing in a head race, it might be best for bow to steer. He will have to turn and look anyway, so he may as well have control over the course. In this situation the boat will be constantly changing direction, so the stroke will not be able to steer off a point lined up with the sternpost.

Once you have decided who is going to do it, steering a sculling boat is relatively easy. Most crews seem to prefer no rudder to steering with a rudder. Asking teammates to pull harder on port or starboard seems a lot easier. Moreover, it isn't as easy to oversteer using blade pressure. If your course is analogous to a snake's, you can blame it on the inability of your teammates to follow orders.

That being said, there is one instance where you should seriously consider using a rudder. Head races on particularly twisty courses can be much simpler to steer if you have a rudder to help you navigate especially tight turns. I speak from experience, having hit two bridges and one boat while racing the double at the Head of the Charles.

If you do choose to use a rudder (usually attached to cables running to a footstretcher), make sure you cross the cables before you connect them to the rudder. This makes steering a no-brainer; you simply point your foot in the direction you'd like to go. There are a couple of rules you should follow. First, steer only while the blades are in the water. The boat is much more unstable when the oars are out of the water on the recovery, and the balance can be easily affected by even a slight course correction. Second, try for slight course corrections instead of less frequent but major changes in direction. It is easy to oversteer when using a rudder, and many a bowman has found himself fishtailing wildly across the river, a victim of acute oversteer.

DOUBLES

Rowing a double is quite a bit different from a single. In fact, due to the nature of the boat a double may be the most difficult boat to row well. There are a number of complicating factors to contend with, which are either boat-related or sculler-related.

A double is significantly faster then a single. This additional speed means reaction times are decreased, races are shorter so you have to execute your race plan in less time, and you have to row at a higher rating, increase the load on your oars, or both. Sculler-related considerations merit close attention in the double. It is rare for two evenly matched scullers to row a double together, so almost inevitably you will find yourself matched up with someone who is better than you in some respects and weaker in others. Technically, these differences can all be accommodated. The hard part is to deal with these relative differences in a positive and mature way. It is all too easy to rationalize a bad piece or practice by focusing on the mistakes, real or imagined, your partner made. This doesn't accomplish anything.

Some scullers are resistant to making changes in their style to help a double blend together. There are two factors to consider in this situation. First, is your technique really that good? Second, where does the double fit on your list of priorities? If the real answer to the first question is yes and the second is not very high, you may find the double to be a frustrating experience. If you are in the double because it's February and you are reluctant to row the single until the water warms up, no problem. If you plan on racing the double, make sure you and your partner understand the implications your attitude has on your chances of success.

Doubles are fun to row only when you realize you and your partner each have flaws and you focus on correcting your own errors and allow your partner to do the same. Doubles are not fun to row when each sculler harps on the other's problems throughout the practice. Each double will probably go through a period when all the problems are due to the other guy's imperfections. The best way to get through these periods is to agree to leave technical discussions for the dock. This will (hopefully) allow each sculler to focus on his own problems, secure in the knowledge that the other is doing the same.

A videotape is the impartial third party that you can use to arbitrate disagreements and identify problem areas. If you can get a workout taped every two weeks or so, you'll be able to precisely identify individual imperfections and points in the stroke cycle where the two scullers aren't in sync. Of course, the video should be used as a training aid, not as a confirmation of your partner's poor technique. If possible, review the tape with a coach or experienced sculler who can help you recognize technical flaws and recommend solutions.

Setting the Lineup

The question of who should stroke and who should bow can be a difficult one to answer, but there are a couple of guidelines that may make the decision easier. If you are putting together a crew for a race and have little chance to practice together, say between the dock and the starting line, put the most adaptable sculler in the bow.

The most important technical consideration in a double is to row together. You will go faster if you are rowing imperfectly but together than if one of you insists on rowing correctly. Regardless of other considerations such as height, weight, aggressiveness, or experience, the sculler who will adapt best to the other's unique style should sit in the bow.

For those of you who will have an opportunity to actually practice together a few times before race day, the decision gets a little more complicated. There are several factors you should consider before deciding who sits where, including relative size, experience, aggressiveness, steering ability, and technical ability. No one factor is the most important single criterion, rather they all contribute to the decision. The decision comes down to how the boat feels and how fast it goes.

A rule of thumb says the bigger sculler sits in the stern. This helps get the bow out of the water, reducing the amount of friction created by the hull moving through the water. The importance of size in the decision is in direct proportion to

Make sure you look around often. A double's speed will bring you up on other boats faster than you realize.

An example of rowing together. The catch is a little violent for a double, but the crew will be faster catching together and hard than if one sculler catches correctly.

the difference in relative size between the two scullers. If you outweigh your partner by 40 pounds, you should strongly consider sitting in the stroke seat.

There are good reasons for putting the more experienced sculler in the bow as well as in the stern. The bowman usually steers, gives commands, and calls the race plan, a job of some importance. Obviously the more experienced the sculler, the more comfortable he should be with these tasks. On the other hand, the stroke must set and maintain the pace, a stressful and demanding role that can be quite difficult in a close race.

The more experience the sculler has, the more likely he is to perform well under pressure. The key is to put the experienced sculler where he will do the most good and put the less-experienced sculler where he will do the least harm.

Psychologically, the role of the stroke is a demanding one. The ideal stroke is the sculler who can remain calm and collected in the heat of competition, following the race strategy exactly as planned.

The place for an aggressive sculler is the stroke seat. A common saying in the sport is great strokes are born, not made.

A determined, aggressive, self-confident stroke who loves to win can make a decent crew a lot better. This is especially true in a double, where this attitude is relatively easy to transmit to the bowman. The aggressive stroke will know when it's time to forget the race plan and do whatever it takes to win the race, a skill that cannot be taught. As he is setting the pace, the bow has no choice but to save his breath and follow along.

Probably the most common way of determining the lineup is to put the one who can steer in the appropriate seat. Not the most logical way to do things, but it saves wear and tear on the brain tissue. In actuality, this is probably one of the less important factors to consider. With a little practice and a little patience, almost anyone can steer from the stroke or bow seat.

Just because someone hasn't done it before doesn't mean they can't. Try using blade pressure instead of a rudder to steer. If you absolutely have to, use a rudder; otherwise avoid it.

Technique is like experience in that there are just as many reasons to put the technician in bow as in stroke. A good technical sculler in bow will make for a better balanced boat with little or no sterncheck, two key features that will allow the stroke to concentrate on the rate and race plan. Another argument for better technique in the bow is he will be able to coach the stroke and help improve his technique. This is a somewhat shaky argument because the stroke may not be interested in being coached, at least not by the bowman.

If the bowman is the type who can learn by example, he may benefit from sculling behind a technically competent stroke. Moreover, a sculler who tends to rush the slide should probably not stroke, as this tendency will slow down the boat almost as efficiently as throwing out an anchor. Another flaw you should not ignore is a slow catch. Interestingly, scullers who rush the slide often hang at the catch as well.

Finally, a lineup is never carved in stone. It can and should change when conditions dictate or when things just aren't going well. Sometimes it can be helpful to switch positions just to get a different perspective on things and make a practice a little different.

Rigging

Rigging a double is not just a case of increasing the load on the same oars you use in the single. There are a number of factors to consider, but the most important is to rig the boat so the oars go in the water at the same time and release the water at the same time. Any other changes you may make will not have the same influence on boat speed as simply making sure you are in time with your partner.

Given the variety of body types presently occupying doubles, this relatively simple concept can be quite difficult in execution and often requires a lot of trial and error before the best rig is found. Before you start making major changes to the rig, remember the basic rule of rigging: one change at a time. If you try to do everything at once, you'll have no idea why it feels better or worse and you will be no better off than before.

The other basic rule of rigging also applies to rigging a double: start out with a standard rig based on your present level of ability and make changes from there. Even if your aspirations are to make the Olympic team, don't try to row with the same rig they do until you are ready.

The most important step is the next one. Go out and row, doing a number of different pieces at varying pressures and over different distances. If possible, have someone accompany you in a launch and watch the timing and angle of the oars at the catch and the release. If they are able to videotape, so much the better.

The oars should move as if they were tied together, catching and releasing the water at precisely the same moment. Chances are the timing is a little off. This is where the video comes in. More often than not, some part of the mistiming is due to mistakes in technique, not rigging. Before you start fooling with the rigging, consult the video to make sure you aren't trying to solve style problems by rigging around them. If you don't have a video, you'll have to listen to the observer in the launch, a poor substitute but certainly better than relying on your instincts.

In most cases one of the scullers in a double will be stronger and one will have a longer reach. The stronger sculler will get the oars through the water faster than the weaker sculler, and the sculler with the longer reach will spend more time with his oars in the water than his partner. Do not make the mistake of assuming a shorter sculler rows a shorter stroke than a taller one. In many cases shorter scullers have adopted an extremely long stroke in an effort to fit into crews populated with tall, gangly types. The distance from the catch to the release is what is important here, not the height of the sculler.

If the sculler with the short reach is also the stronger one, simply increase his work by adjusting the span, the inboard, or both. This will move the pivot point in closer to the sculler, increasing his angle at the catch, at the finish, and simultaneously decreasing his leverage. The opposite approach will work for the taller and weaker sculler. This process is a series of small steps resulting in a compromise. In most situations, each sculler's rig will be adjusted slightly so neither has to row with too severe a rig.

If the sculler with the longer reach is also stronger, the solution may become more complicated. In most cases, these two differences will cancel each other, so he will simply row a longer stroke than his partner and compensate by pulling the oars through the water faster. The result is a well-matched crew. In particularly mismatched doubles, the timing still may not be right. Try to change the inboard measurement relative to the span to compensate. You two just may not be the right combination for a double.

Since most double combinations are not perfectly matched, you'll probably find one of you has a longer reach and the only way to make the catch and release line up perfectly is for one of you to shorten up, the other to overreach, or both. If the problem is mild don't change your technique; the solution might be worse than the problem. To correct egregious errors, try re-setting the footstretchers or changing the through-the-pin measurements.

Racing

The most important thing in racing a double is for you and your partner to be in complete agreement about the race plan, goals, tactics, and emergency plans. After you have agreed to work together and before you actually work up a race plan, consider a couple of facts about the double.

First, it is faster and feels lighter. A higher rating, a heavier workload, or both is called for. A double is raced at least two strokes higher than a single, and often more than that. Second, because the double is a faster boat, the race is over faster. Some scullers make the mistake of running out of race course because the race goes by so fast. Be aware of what is happening and where you are during a race and respond accordingly.

There are a couple of additional recommendations I can make regarding racing a double. First, practice the race plan, especially the start. If you and your partner are primarily single scullers, your starting styles may be completely different. Make sure you are rowing the start in time and with the same motion. It is common for crews to lose a length or more at the start because of lousy technique; don't put yourself in the position of having to make up two and a half seconds due to inadequate preparation.

Note that the catch angles are identical.

Both scullers appear to be overreaching slightly. In this case the crew is best left alone, since changing one sculler's technique would slow the boat.

Second, learn your strengths and weaknesses and those of your partner. Consider them carefully when devising a racing strategy; don't just do the race plan you always do. If you are a good starter and your partner is better in the middle 1000, compromise by going out a little slower so you can keep up with him when you normally would be hitting the wall.

Finally, if you'll be rowing in head races, learn the course and learn it well. Go over it several times in the boat, walk the course together and discuss how you'll handle problem areas. Again, the idea is to gain confidence by knowing what to do and when to do it.

QUADS

If you are primarily a single sculler, you'll find a quad difficult to steer and very fast, and you may have a tough time deciding where you should sit and who will call the practices and races.

Conversely, if you aren't known as the technician around the boathouse and you find singles frustrating because you have to think too much, the quad could be the boat for you. You can get away with merely adequate sculling in a quad because it is easier to hide poor technique among four than between two. Quads are also a lot easier to balance than doubles and a lot more comfortable in rough water.

Quads are just like doubles only more so. They are very fast, making steering even more interesting. They don't turn quickly, but seem to keep turning forever. With two more seats to fill, seating decisions can be significantly more complicated, with a number of factors contributing to that complexity.

Much of the discussion pertaining to doubles also is relevant to quads and therefore doesn't need repeating. If your interest is strictly quad sculling, read the section on double sculling anyway.

Rigging

Rigging a quad is completely different from a double or single. Due to its high power-to-weight ratio and the larger blade space, a quad is almost as fast as an eight and is quicker off the start. If you try to use the oars you use in the single in a quad, you'll find yourself windmilling through the water.

You will probably get better results using oars that are slightly longer than single sculling blades; two centimeters seems to be about right. Set up the inboard measurement using standard rigging measurements and make changes from there to account for tall, short, strong, or not-so-strong members of the crew.

Again, try to make sure any changes you make to individuals' rigging are due to factors beyond the sculler's control. Try hard to avoid solving technique problems by rigging around them.

Setting the Lineup

Things can get a little more complicated here just because you have two more people to deal with; along with their technical idiosyncrasies you will have to factor in their emotional characteristics. Some scullers just can't handle the responsibility

A bowman's view of a heavyweight quad. Mark Borchelt photo.

of bow or stroke and are much happier sitting in the middle of the boat pulling hard. If you come across one or two of these stoic types, rejoice. Unfortunately, most scullers think they can stroke a boat better than anybody else, so your chances of actually finding folks content to sit in the middle of the boat may not be too high.

As in any other boat, the bowman plays an important role in balancing the boat, steering, and maintaining good slide control. If you have a person with all these attributes who also happens to be the lightest person on the squad, you have the ideal bowman. Bow's technical expertise is critical to the success of the boat. A common expression in rowing is a rushed slide starts from the bow. Everyone else in the boat can feel the bowman rushing the slide and often speeds his slide as well. The result is little run from the boat, a high rating, and a tendency to run out of gas before the end of the piece. Seek out a sculler with a slow slide for the bow seat.

Technical skill is not only slide control; bladework is also a significant factor in selecting the bowman. A sculler with sloppy bladework who is always getting caught at the finish will drag the boat down to one side or the other, frustrating the daylights out of his teammates. Put your best sculler in the bow and the rest of you can concentrate on pulling hard.

The engine room, or middle of the boat, is comprised of the two and three seats. These scullers are there to move the boat, not to steer, devise race strategy, or set the rating. Engine room occupants are generally bigger and stronger than the bow, and often they stroke as well. Technique, while important, is not as vital as strength and conditioning.

The two seat brings to mind a common expression in rowing. If you rowed in eights in college, you probably heard the coach or a teammate say the next seat after the three seat is the launch. The two seat in the quad is analogous to the three seat in an eight; the least-skilled sculler is hidden there where he can do the least amount of damage. If he does start to slow the rest of the boat down, he will likely find himself sitting in the launch while someone else occupies the two seat.

The three man is usually the biggest and strongest person in the boat. To use the sweep rowing analogy again, the comparable seat in the eight would be six. His primary function is to support the stroke rating with aggressive rowing right in sync with the stroke. An effective three man will help the stroke maintain a rating without rushing the slide or doing anything else to disrupt the boat's run.

Just as in the double, the stroke's role is to set and maintain the appropriate stroke rating by sculling aggressively and with a controlled recovery. He should have a lot of confidence in his abilities and the abilities of his teammates, confidence that will enable him to handle unique or high-pressure situations without panicking and abandoning the race plan. This confidence will enable the crew to recover from a crab, collision, or other mishap quickly and efficiently, and is especially important when rowing against another crew that does the unexpected.

Racing

If you and your teammates are serious about the quad, spend enough time in it to get comfortable. Racing a quad is more like racing in an eight than a single. The boat is big, very fast, and chances are you don't have to think as much as you would in a single. At least you don't have to think about as many things.

The only part of the race where you can move a length or more on your competitors without killing yourself is the start. It is a lot harder to make up a length in the body of the race, especially in a quad. If you think about the amount of time you spend training to pick up a boat length over the course of the race, the amount of time most crews invest in learning how to get away from the stakeboats quickly and cleanly is negligible. Make some time to work on the start. Have someone watch you to make sure everyone is in time, catching and releasing in sync; work on getting the hands out of bow quickly and cleanly to get the rating up in the first few strokes.

If your quad is comprised of single scullers or is an amalgamation of scullers thrown together for a race, make sure you spend a good amount of time developing an effective settle.

If your settle is confused or disorganized, your quad will lose ground due to poor technique and you stand a good chance of becoming rattled, hurting your performance for the rest of the race. Some scullers like to settle in two or three strokes, others in one, some take the slide down, others slow the hands. Decide how you are going to settle and practice it until you have it down cold.

The sprint at the end of the race or, for that matter, any sprint can cause problems for the ill-prepared crew. Again, decide what the race plan is, when and how you're going to make your move, and practice it well. You might want to refer to the chapter on racing the single for a more detailed discussion of the settle, the sprint, and other race tactics.

Head Racing

Rowing a head race in a quad is an interesting experience, especially for the visiting crew. The bowman, since he's got the best view of the course, should steer unless he is absolutely incapable of telling port from starboard. A rudder is essential—it provides another means of controlling what can be a very difficult boat to steer.

Don't be too leery of going out hard and high in a quad head race because the race is so much shorter than it would be in a single. If you are in any kind of shape, you should be able to maintain the higher pace for the entire three miles. The key is to make sure the hands are coming out of bow fast and smooth; this will maintain a high rating and help prevent rushing the slide.

OCTUPLES

The octuple is a lot of fun to row. It is the fastest thing on the water, very quick off the starting line, and a lot more sociable than any other boat a sculler may find himself in.

Almost everything one would need to know about the octuple has been discussed in some detail in the sections on double and quad sculling. If you are putting a lineup together, put the good scullers in bow and stroke and the heaviest people in five and six. Fill in the rest of the boat by putting scullers in seats they want to sit in. Finally, get a coxswain. Don't even think about trying to scull an octuple without one.

Racing an octuple is simply a matter of starting fast and staying in time. Make sure you are rigged very heavy, and don't worry about race strategy. You won't have time to implement any grandiose plans anyway.

Chapter Twelve

Masters

he popularity of sculling among people over thirty has grown tremendously in recent years. These scullers, considered masters due to their advanced age, range from former national team members to athletes who first picked up a set of oars long after their hair disappeared.

Evidence of this growing popularity can be seen in the numbers competing in masters events. The first masters regatta in the United States was held in 1979 and saw 58 men and no women competing in a variety of events. Only two years later, 378 men and 39 women raced at the Masters National Championships, and the numbers have been growing by leaps and bounds ever since. There is even a world championship regatta for masters that is quite well-attended. On the local level, almost all summer regattas and fall head races include several categories for masters. The growing interest in physical fitness, at least among the economically fortunate people in this country and abroad, has also had a positive effect on the popularity of sculling. For many folks, sculling is a relatively safe, pleasant, and vigorous sport with little chance of injury. Sculling's romantic appeal has also snared a few people who fall for the "it looks so easy and peaceful" image and see themselves out on the water communing with nature, lowering their stress levels before (or after) joining battle with the complicated world they live in. Other, more practical people see sculling as a way to maintain or improve their health without the pounding of running or the expense of the latest fitness fad.

Finally, some people keep sculling because they just get better and better every year. These scullers are confirmation of many studies that show athletic performance does not have to decline with age, only with inactivity.

AGING

Scientific study has found that there are several biological changes that inevitably occur due to aging. Maximal heart rate decreases as does maximal stroke volume (amount of blood the heart can pump in one contraction), so the ability of the heart to supply blood to working muscles and organs decreases. By age 70 this decrease amounts to about a third of the heart's original capability. Lung capacity also declines by a little over a third between the ages of 30 and 70. The effect of these two events is a theoretical decrease in the aerobic capacity of the athlete by about eight to ten percent per decade after the age of 30.

Anaerobic power also decreases with age, as does strength and power. Age's most notable effect is on reaction time, explosive power, quickness, and the ability to change direction rapidly. Although explosive power is important to scullers, on the whole the effect of a diminished capability in these areas is not terribly significant.

Other physiological attributes that are affected by age include the amount of time needed to recover from injury, your basal metabolic rate, which can drop by as much as 25 percent, and thermoregulation efficiency. Now, all this bad news must be kept in perspective.

Most of the studies on aging and its effects on athletic performance are very limited because there have not been many older athletes to study. A lot of the information regarding older athletes is based on the biological changes that occur when average people get older. If you are an older sculler, these studies may have very little meaning for or applicability to you, because they are based on what happens when people who get little exercise continue that behavior as they age. If you think about it in that light, you will quickly realize that it is no wonder these inert folks deteriorate; they do nothing to prevent it.

The other problem with many of these studies is they use a "snapshot" of selected older athletes rather than tracking their performance over a long period to see what changes actually occur. If you don't actually know what an athlete was capable of in his youth, you have no way of knowing if his present performance level is better, worse, or identical to that previous level. Without longitudinal study (a study of the same population over a long period) any statements about change in performance due to the effects of aging are pure conjecture and must be treated as such.

Recent studies, both longitudinal and specific, raise serious questions about the accuracy of some of the earlier assessments of the effects of aging on physiological abilities. For example, a 1986 study by the National Institute of Aging, which assessed 120 senior athletes, most older than 60, found that, "these highly motivated athletes . . . possess maximal aerobic capacities comparable to those observed in healthy 25-year-old athletes." Michael Pollock, the director of the University of Florida's Center for Exercise Science, found that several athletes he has studied (all older than 50) lost only 4 to 5 percent of their aerobic capacity in the course of a decade—half of what one would expect. Moreover, some of the subjects showed no measurable decrease in aerobic capacity. The apparent reason for this continued good health may lie in the amount and the intensity of exercise performed by the subjects; they averaged 35 miles of running per week, a pretty healthy load. If you want to perform at a high level, you can probably maintain a level of performance very close to your best effort as a mere youth, but you are going to have to work very hard.

Since aging takes its toll primarily in strength, coordination, reaction time, and power, athletes competing in endurance events, skill events, or events like sculling that incorporate both, are going to lose less of the critical abilities that have made them successful in the past. Moreover, some of the loss of power and speed may be a function of insufficient time spent training rather than physiological deterioration.

If you have been rowing for some time, you'll find yourself better prepared mentally than when you were younger and physiologically better fit. The more experience you have, the better prepared you will be to handle the pressures and stress of training, the smarter you will train, and the more intelligently you will race. This comes from knowing yourself; you've already made the mistakes and know what you can and cannot do. Since so much of sculling is mental, you are probably better off with the experience provided by age than the (questionably) better physiological abilities associated with youth.

INJURIES

From personal experience I can say it takes longer to recover—both from injuries and workouts—at 32 years old that it did when I was 20. I also have to be more cautious and make sure I listen to my body very closely. It just doesn't pay to shrug off seemingly minor pains or aches; too often they signal something more serious that comes out if I am not more careful. Other than the recovery time and less time to work out, not much else has changed.

Most of the injuries suffered by masters stem from overuse. Bursitis, infected blisters, strained muscles, and sore backs are all common injuries associated with too much work too soon for muscles that are not yet ready for the stress. Masters may need to pay special attention to injuries, weather, and the way they feel, especially if they have a past history of medical problems.

One physiological factor that merits attention is the cardiovascular system. The health of the cardiovascular system will have more impact on your ability to handle the stresses from sculling than any other single factor. This is especially true with regard to environmental considerations such as heat and cold. If your heart has been weakened due to hypertension, atherosclerosis, or ischemia (past heart attacks), it will be less able to respond to the increased demands placed on it in the event you flip in cold water or get dehydrated in the heat of summer. This doesn't mean you can't scull, but it does mean that if you don't take precautions, you may end your sculling days prematurely.

More specifically, if you have atherosclerosis you may be at particularly high risk in hot weather. Your body transfers excessive heat from the core to the surface; if the blood flow is restricted your ability to transfer heat can be seriously impaired. Be careful and prudent if your physician has told you your blood pressure is higher than it should be.

Some of the injuries you may encounter are described in the chapter on exercise physiology. Although none of them are unique to masters, you'll be more suscep- tible to them than the kids and the injuries will lay you up longer. Many of the examples cited are caused by improper technique, as are almost all sculling-related injuries. In all cases you may heal the injury but unless you figure out what is causing the problem, you will reinjure yourself as soon as you get back into the boat.

One "injury," osteoarthritis, is more commonly seen in masters than among the general population. Osteoarthritis often affects the lower back. Its symptoms include a sharp, deep muscular pain as the back's muscles struggle to protect the weakened spine. Osteoarthritis can usually be identified by X-ray; treatment is best left to a physician or chiropractor. Osteoarthritis should not prevent you from sculling although it may limit the amount and intensity of sculling you are able to do comfortably.

If you do get hurt—no matter what the cause—take the time to analyze the injury. Find out what may have caused it: Was it a flaw in your technique? Or perhaps you were saving a few minutes by not stretching or warming up before the workout. If your technique looks fine, the cause of the injury may be related to muscular weakness. In this case you may want to see a physical therapist or physician to accurately assess the cause.

If you are serious about your sculling, find a good doctor. Don't go to one who treats sick people, find one who is used to dealing with athletes, one who will understand your sport, your commitment, and the mental stresses that are associated with physical injuries. You may find a chiropractor to be useful; they are trained to look for the root cause of the problem and advise you on steps you can take to eliminate the cause of the problem. Other physicians may treat the symptoms instead of the problem itself. No matter who you work with ask a lot of questions and make sure you understand the answers.

The only thing that will slow you down as you age is yourself. Although there is inevitable deterioration in some aspects of physical performance as a result of aging, the negative effects of aging are more than offset by the knowledge gained from many miles, many races, and much training. When it is hard to believe that, take solace in the fact that your competitors are just as old as you are. You do not have to accept the inevitable effects of maturity if you don't want to.

TRAINING AND CONDITIONING

The biggest obstacle encountered by master scullers is finding and keeping the time you need to train. With so many other important considerations, it is especially important that you set up a training program, keep a log, and periodically evaluate your progress.

If you are creative and plan ahead, you can minimize the disruption caused by other things infringing on your sculling. If you can't make it to the water, do your workout on the erg. If you have to go to Toledo on business, bring your workout gear, check into a hotel with lots of floors, and run stairs. If you know you may have to be somewhere during your normal afternoon workout time, get up early and scull before work or before the kids get up. If you really want to make the time, you can.

Occasionally things come up that are unavoidable. When this does happen, do not fall into the compulsive-obsessive guilt trip; berating yourself because you miss workouts is not going to make you any faster and is likely to have the opposite effect. There are some things in life that, on occasion, are more important than sculling. Keep things in perspective.

Before you begin training, make sure you are in decent health. If you have to see a doctor to determine this, go ahead. This is especially important if you are male, over 35, and have not been exercising on a regular (two or three times a week) basis. Women might want to see their doctors before they begin working out if they are over 40 and have not participated in a regular exercise program recently. Of course, if you smoke, are overweight, have high blood pressure, absolutely do not start any kind of exercise program without first seeing a physician.

Be careful with your preparation, train smart, and you'll never notice you aren't 20 any more. Perhaps the most important thing you can do is make sure you spend sufficient time warming up; since age increases your chances of injury and injuries take longer to heal, you want to reduce your chances of getting hurt as much as possible.

This preparation starts with the first workout of the season. If you are just getting into sculling or are getting back into shape after a layoff, start off slow and easy; you'll have plenty of opportunity to exhaust yourself later on when you get into the intense part of your training schedule.

The first three to four weeks should be used to get the muscles and joints ready for more rigorous training. Make sure you stretch; don't think you can skip stretching and get away with it. You may for a day or a few days, but one day you will hurt yourself badly because you are trying to save a few minutes. Body circuits will help stretch the muscles and connective tissue, which tends to lose its elasticity with age. Along with body circuits and stretching, do aerobic workouts three times a week for the first three weeks, keeping the intensity level fairly low. At this point in your season you are not trying to get in shape for sculling, you are getting in shape to get in shape.

Once you have your base established, get into a routine. If you are focusing on 1000 meter races, emphasize anaerobic training. If you are aiming for head races, spend most of your time with anaerobic threshold work, endurance training, and a little interval work to keep the intensity level up. Leave most of the competition to the race course; although a workout a couple times a week with friends will keep you sharp, you don't want to get caught up in the excitement at the expense of your carefully planned schedule. It doesn't make any sense to try to beat someone in practice if you are supposed to be concentrating on endurance training for that workout. Save your competitive juices for the real thing.

There are a few guidelines to keep in mind as you develop your plan for the season. First, think back on seasons past (if there were any) and recall when you felt least like sculling during the season. This exercise may help you identify the cause or causes of your dissatisfaction or burn-out. Factor these causes into your planning. Next, select an event you wish to peak for and the stroke rate you plan on using for that event. Now plan backwards.

If you want to race at 33 strokes per minute on July 30, plan on rowing no higher than a 31 throughout June, a 29 in May, and a 28 or thereabouts in April. Stick to these ratings throughout the month; they will feel high and uncomfortable the first few pieces of the month but by the last week you will find you have adapted quite well to the higher stroke.

To get used to the higher rating and build your comfort level, only try for the target rating during short pieces, say under a minute or 30 strokes during the first week. The second week you can incorporate the target rating into your 500-meter pieces, the third week you'll be sculling at the target rate for an entire 1000 meter piece, and by the last week the target rate will be suitable for your shorter anaerobic threshold work. As you get further into the season you will find it harder and harder to get comfortable at the higher target rate, but by pushing your limits gradually you'll be able to iron out any technical flaws in your stroke before you try to row any higher.

Try to scull four or five times per week. More often than that probably isn't sustainable without straining your professional or personal life and you'll just get depressed when the unavoidable occurs and you have to cut back. Be realistic.

During the week you should vary the intensity of your workouts to allow your body a chance to recover and build strength and stamina. Remember, your body only gets better when you allow it to rest and recover. You can get the rest either by alternating hard and easy (half pressure or less) days or by using a slightly more complicated schedule of easy, medium, off, easy, medium, hard, off. Play around with both scenarios and find the one you like best, or just alternate between them. Whatever you decide, codify it in your written plan and record the results in your logbook.

RACE STRATEGIES

It is certainly not any easier to race 1000 meters than it is to race 2000, and in fact it can be even more painful because it requires a larger contribution from your anaerobic energy systems. At present there is an ongoing debate concerning the proper distance for masters races. Some favor the standard 2000 meters and some the traditional masters distance of 1000. The longer distance places less of a strain on the cardiovascular system. The 1000-meter distance, which is presently the official distance, creates a higher concentration of lactic acid in the blood and muscles that the cardiovascular system must rid itself of.

The difficulty with the 1000 meters is you end up rowing at a pace that is considerably above your anaerobic threshold for most of the race. Moreover, you don't get a chance to establish a solid race cadence; it seems just as you are getting into the settle and approaching a (physiological) steady state, the finish line appears out of the corner of your eye and it's time to start taking the rating up.

This shorter distance gives an advantage to the power-oriented scullers over the endurance types. Also, the even-splits strategy has less applicability because there is less time for oxygen debt, lactic-acid buildup, and the other effects of anaerobic respiration to become factors.

Practically, this means if you want to go out high and hard, you will still incur a large oxygen debt. However, you will only have to carry this debt for less than 1000 meters. If you have a great start, you may be able to get enough of a lead to put the race out of reach of your competitors. The key will be to get out in front, settle, relax, and concentrate on sculling well. As you have nothing left to sprint with, you better make sure every stroke between the settle and the finish is as efficient as possible.

If your strategy is to maintain an even pace for the distance, settle hard and high. You don't have much time to overtake the race leaders, so start pushing the pace as soon as possible. Again, relax on the recovery and concentrate on your own sculling. If you concentrate on your opponents, you may find yourself panicking because you aren't moving on them as fast as you would like. This is only good news for them, so keep your head in your own boat.

In the four minutes or so it takes to cover 1000 meters, it is also more difficult to relax and focus on the task at hand. Since you have less time to compensate for any mistakes when problems arise, the tendency is to panic and become frantic. You may find yourself thinking about the poor start you had or the little crab you caught when you went through that last wake instead of concentrating on the next stroke. Save the analysis for the ride home; during the race, focus on the strokes yet to come.

One of the interesting things about masters sculling is the time credits given according to the age of the participants. If you are relatively young, you may beat an older sculler by several lengths only to find yourself getting the silver. Another example of the benefits of doing your homework. If you know how much of a time advantage the other scullers in your race have, you'll be able to accurately assess your real position during the race and make adjustments accordingly.

There are several different categories into which mature scullers fall. The categories vary from regatta to regatta depending on participation levels, so be sure you have the right classification before you send in the entry form. The USRA's standard handicap chart is provided below for your edification. Since many regattas don't have enough participants (yet) to fill the eight categories, the categories you may find at your local regatta may bear little resemblance to the handicap table that follows.

Age handicaps.

Category	Ages	Yrs/Cat	Seconds/Yr	Seconds/Cat
A	27–35	9	0.5	4.5
B	36–42	7	1.0	7.0
C	43–49	7	1.3	9.1
D	50–54	5	1.5	7.5
E	55–59	5	1.7	8.5
F	60–64	5	1.9	9.5
G	65–69	5	2.1	10.5
H	70+		2.3	

(June 1990 *Rowing Report*.)

Category: Masters are divided into eight age categories
Ages: As of December 31 of the current year
Yrs/Cat: Number of years included in that category
Seconds/Yr: Number of seconds allowed for each year over the initial year in that
category; aka the handicap
Seconds/Cat: Total seconds of handicap within that age category (Yrs/Cat
multiplied by Seconds/Yr)

Make the most of your time by planning intelligently, setting priorities, and keeping a logbook. And don't get too intense about it. Make sure you enjoy everything about masters' sculling, especially the activities surrounding the event.

Sources

The United States Rowing Association is the national governing body for rowing and sculling. It sponsors regattas, hires national team coaches, publishes newsletters and the magazine *American Rowing*, sets the rules, and represents the sport's interests. The USRA was originally known as the National Association of Amateur Oarsmen, but progress and the women's movement forced the name change to the definitely less-romantic USRA. The USRA can be found at 201 S. Capitol Street, Suite 400, Indianapolis, IN 46225. One of the USRA's corporate sponsors, Audi of America, funds a toll-free information line; the number is 1-800-OAR-AUDI. For more information on sculling call The Rower's Bookshelf in Essex, MA, at 508-468-4096.

Sculling Schools

The number of sculling schools has grown substantially over the last few years. A few are listed below; no costs or schedules are listed as these are subject to change. Overall, the costs are quite reasonable and some have excellent, world-class coaching. When you call these schools be explicit about your interest and experience level. If you are not sure what level you have attained, discuss your needs and expectations with the school staff before you sign up. If you fail to, you may find yourself out of your league.

Craftsbury Sculling Center
Box 31-R, Craftsbury Common, VT, 05827
Tel. 802-586-7767
Head Coach: Steve Wagner
The original sculling school, started in the mid-seventies. Craftsbury also runs camps for other sports for those couples with diverse interests. Craftsbury also uses a number of visiting coaches, so you may want to schedule your trip around their coaching schedule. Programs run May through October.

Durham Boat Company Sculling School
264 Newmarket Road, Durham, NH, 03824
Tel. 603-659-2548
Head Coach: Jim Dreher, 1990 U.S. Men's National Lightweight Sculling Team coach
One of Jim's crews won the gold at the World Championships in 1990. He is perhaps the best sculling coach in the country. Operates in Florida in the winter months and in Durham, New Hampshire in the summer.

Florida Rowing Center
1140 Fifth Avenue, New York, NY, 10128
Tel. 212-996-1196
Director: Peter Sparhawk.
Sessions run continuously from November through May.

Northeast Sculling School
P.O. Box 2060, Duxbury, Massachusetts 02331
Tel. 617-934-6192
Several coaches available.
One one-week session in the summer, school is located in Kents Hill, Maine.

Open Water Rowing
85 Libertyship Way, Sausalito, CA 94965
Tel. 415-332-1091

Quebec Sculling School
3114 rue Marcel Proust, St. Augustin de Desmaures
Quebec, Canada G3A 1X1
Director: Henry Hamilton; other coaches available.
Sessions run from June through mid-September.

Sparhawk Sculling School
Colchester, Vermont, 802-658-4799
West Palm Beach, Florida, 407-798-1093
Head Coach: Peter Sparhawk, retired Princeton University head coach.
May through October in Vermont; October through May in Florida.

If you're not looking for coaching but want to scull someplace warm in the winter, the University of Tampa has facilities you may be able to take advantage of. Call the Facility Rental Department at 813-235-6238 for more information. The water is pretty good and the river is interesting, but you may want to time your visit to miss the college crews who swoop down on Tampa for spring break.

Equipment

The following list is by no means comprehensive. For additional manufacturers you may want to contact the USRA at the address provided above. With a few exceptions, specific boat models have not been provided because they tend to change fairly often.

Some manufacturers offer several models; others limit themselves to one model or class. As product lines are subject to change, please contact the manufacturer directly for a current catalogue or brochure.

Coffey Racing Shells
918 Addison Road
Painted Post, NY 14870
Tel. 607-962-1982
All types of shells and rowing machines

Concept II, Inc.
RR1 Box-1100
Morrisville, VT 05661
Tel. 802-888-7971
Oars, rowing machines, and oarlocks

Durham Boat Company
RFD 2, Newmarket Road
Durham, NH 03824
Tel. 603-659-2548
Full line of racing and recreational shells including team boats and oars

Felker Boat Company
Austin, TX
Tel. 512-288-0734
Racing and recreational shells

R.E. Graham Corporation
Rte. 2, 2351 Highway 28
Quincy, WA 98848
Tel. 800-354-5410

Hudson Racing Shells
RR3
Komoka, Ontario,
CANADA NOL 1RO
Tel. 519-473-9864
Oars and shells

Kaschper Racing Shells, Ltd.
P.O. Box 40
Lucan, Ontario, CANADA
NOM 2JO
Tel. 519-227-4652
Racing singles, doubles, and quads

Little River Marine
P.O. Box 986-C
Gainesville, FL 32602
Tel. 904-378-5025

Maas Boat Company
1453 Harbour Way South
Richmond, CA 95804
Tel. 415-232-1612

Martin Marine
Box 251-A
Kittery Point, ME 03905
Tel. 207-439-1507
Models - Alden Ocean Shell, Martin Trainer

Owen Racing Shells
1307 Clark Mill Road
Sweet Home, OR 97386
Tel. 503-367-6976
Racing singles and doubles

Peinert Boatworks
52 Coffin Avenue
New Bedford, MA 02476
Tel. 508-990-0105
Racing and recreational singles

Pocock Racing Shells
2212 Pacific Avenue
Everett, WA 98201
Tel. 206-252-6658

Empacher
13 Donezette St.
Wellesly, MA 02181
Tel. 617-239-0571

Van Dusen Racing Boats
aka Composite Engineering
277 Baker Avenue
Concord, MA 01742
Tel. 508-371-3132
Strictly high-end racing shells

Glossary

aerobic: Literally, "with oxygen"; refers to the use of oxygen to produce energy in the muscle cells.

age: An oft-cited but rarely good reason for poor and slow sculling.

air strokes: Sculling without placing the blades in the water.

Alden: The name given to the original open-water sculling boat. Aldens are excellent for rough water as well as for inexperienced scullers.

alveoli: The tiny air sacs in the lungs where the exchange of gases between the air and the blood occurs.

anaerobic: Literally, "without oxygen"; refers to the two energy systems that produce energy without oxygen in the muscle cell. See also lactic acid and phosphocreatine.

anaerobic threshold: The exertion level at which the athlete begins to significantly increase the use of the anaerobic energy systems. Technically it is now generally accepted that one has "crossed" the anaerobic threshold when the blood lactate level reaches 3-4 mol/liter. A simpler indicator is when you start breathing a lot faster and can no longer carry on a conversation without gasping.

ATP (adenosine triphosphate): The chemical compound that is the basis for all direct energy production in the muscle cell.

ATP-PC system: See phosphagen.

backing it down: Refers to sculling backwards; usually used when landing or pulling into a stakeboat.

backsplash: The splash produced by the blade entering the water at the catch while the blade is moving toward the bow.

blade: Usually refers to the business end of the oar, the wide flat part that contacts the water. Can also refer to the entire oar.

boat: Generic term applied to any sculling or rowing craft as well as any other waterborne vehicle.

Boathouse Row: The row of boathouses along the Schuylkill River in Philadelphia's Fairmont Park that symbolizes club rowing.

bow: The front of the boat.

button: Also known as the collar; this is the ring around the sleeve of the oar that is moved to adjust the inboard.

Canadian Henley: One of the most fun regattas around. Five days of racing in St. Catherine's, Ontario. Races go off every ten minutes all day long, there are real live fans who know what they are watching, and there are a tremendous number of very fast crews from Canadian clubs.

cannon fodder: Slow scullers who don't train and thus get creamed every race.

carbohydrate: One of the basic foodstuffs (including starches, sugars, and cellulose), containing carbon, hydrogen, and oxygen.

carbon fiber: A very strong, very light fibrous material used to add rigidity to hulls, riggers, and oars. Usually black. Also known as graphite.

catch: That part of the stroke cycle where the sculler puts the blades in the water while simultaneously reversing direction on the slide.

club: The focus of sculling after college. The club system revolves around a large number of private organizations set up expressly for the purpose of promulgating the sport.

crab, or catch a crab: What occurs when your oar(s) get stuck in the water at the end of the drive and you cannot get them out without a good deal of effort. Can lead to capsizing.

collar: See button.

coxswain, or cox 'n, or simply cox: The human baggage in sweep boats who exists to tell sweep rowers what to do and when to do it; also steers the boat. Real purpose of this person is hard to discern since scullers perform quite well in his absence.

crossover: The movement of one oar handle over the other during the recovery and drive.

dash: A short and furious sprint featured at major regattas over a quarter-mile or occasionally 500 meters. Great spectator sport but very painful for the participants.

deck: The material covering the top of the bow and stern sections of the boat. Decking can be anything from clear plastic to solid Kevlar.

dehydration: Condition resulting from a water deficit, usually associated with exercise in hot conditions.

Designed Water Line (DWL): The horizontal plane along which the boat is designed to contact the water. In some areas, the DWL can be estimated by observing the scum line along the hull when you lift the boat out of the water.

diaphragm: The muscle running horizontally under the lungs that is used to expand and contract the lungs so you can breathe.

dive: A tendency to try to lean forward, usually in an effort to get extra reach, right at the catch. Diving sinks the boat into the water by transferring weight abruptly into the stern. Also an establishment frequented by scullers because they cannot afford anything more upscale.

double sculls: The technical name for a boat for two scullers; also known as a double.

double-up: To race two events at a regatta.

drill: A series of motions that are performed to reinforce a particular aspect of technique.

drive: That part of the stroke cycle when the blades are in the water.

electron transport system: Part of the aerobic energy system process whereby electrons and hydrogen ions combine to form water, and ATP is resynthesized. Takes place in the mitochondrion.

energy: The ability to perform work.

engine room: The term describing the middle two seats (two and three) in a quad that are usually occupied by the biggest and strongest scullers.

ergometer: A device, such as a rowing machine, used to measure the physiological effects of exercise.

fascia: The transparent, thin membrane surrounding muscle tissue.

fast twitch (FT): Technical term referring to the physiology of a muscle cell, enabling this powerful cell to produce copious amounts of energy quickly.

feather: Rolling the oar handle in your hand so the blade is parallel to the water.

fin: The thin, flat structure protruding from the center of the bottom of the hull about two-thirds of the way toward the stern. Also known as the skeg.

finish: The point in the stroke cycle where the legs are straight and the hands have finished pulling the oars into the body.

finals: The ultimate race in a regatta where the champion is decided.

FISA: The international governing body for the sport.

focus: What you must do if you wish to be a competent sculler.

footstretcher: The part of the internal structure of the boat consisting of a crossmember running from port to starboard between which two shoes or clogs are

fastened and into which you put your feet.

frontstops: The stops in the stern end of the tracks that prevent you from sliding out of the tracks and into the footwell.

glucose: The simple carbohydrate stored in the blood, liver, and muscle in a form known as glycogen.

glycolysis: The initial stage in the breakdown of glycogen; results in pyruvate in the presence of oxygen and lactic acid in the absence of oxygen.

graphite: See carbon fiber.

grip: The rubber or wood part of the oar handle you hold onto when you are sculling.

gunwale: The structure surrounding the cockpit that helps keep water out.

halfpressure: The application of power in a sculling boat such that you are rowing half as hard as you can at full. A pretty vague definition, but the only one that exists. If you are rowing at 70-75 percent of your maximal heart rate you are pretty close.

hang: A technical flaw caused when you get to the catch and pause before you put the blades into the water. Or, a well-executed aspect of technique involving the suspension of one's body weight from the oar handles and the footstretchers, achieving an effective drive.

head race: A race against the clock where crews start at approximately ten second intervals and chase each other up a usually winding river course. The object is to pass and prevent the same from occurring to you.

heats: The initial races you must get through if you are to advance to the finals.

heat cramps: Painful muscular contractions caused by prolonged and excessive exposure to environmental heat.

heat exhaustion: Fatigue, usually severe, caused by prolonged exposure to environmental heat.

heat stroke: A usually fatal result of prolonged exposure to environmental heat, generally associated with insufficient water consumption as well.

hemoglobin: A complex molecule found in red blood cells containing iron and protein. Primary function is to transport oxygen.

Henley: Actually, the Royal Henley Regatta. The third part of the British summer sporting triad. Henley is a series of single-elimination races over a distance of a little over 2100 meters leading up to the championship finals. According to some, it is the ultimate in rowing atmosphere.

high: Term applied to a crew or sculler sculling a large number of strokes per minute; e.g., "Pietra was off the line at a 44; boy, is he rowing high!"

hull: The exterior part of the shell designed to cut through the water.

hypertrophy: The enlargement of a cell or organ, such as a muscle.

imaging: A mental process used to simulate actual muscular movement by performing those actions in the mind.

inboard: The measurement

from the outside of the button to the tip of the handle. Used to determine load.

innervate: The process whereby a nerve causes or has the ability to cause a muscle to perform certain actions.

insurance: Something you should get for your shell. See the USRA for sources.

isokinetic contraction: Contraction in which the tension developed by the muscle while shortening at constant speed is maximal over the full range of motion.

isometric contraction: Contraction where there is no change in the length of a muscle but tension is developed.

isotonic contraction: Contraction where the muscle shortens with varying tension while lifting a constant load. Also referred to as concentric or dynamic contraction.

jump the slide: A problem encountered when the seat comes off the tracks.

jump the start: The act of anticipating the start and leaving the starting line early; may result in penalty or disqualification if you get caught, but you can usually get away with it if you aren't too blatant about it and you do it in the heats.

keeper: Term applying to the gate on the top of the oarlock that you close and lock to keep the oar in place. Also used to refer to the structure on the bottom of the slide that keeps the slide on the tracks.

Kevlar: A trade name referring to a type of very strong and light fiberglass manufactured by the DuPont Company.

knee: The structure in the boat through which the bolts attaching the riggers to the boat pass.

knife: A technical problem encountered when the blade enters the water too deeply, "knifing in."

Krebs cycle: Yet another part of the three-step aerobic energy system process; no ATP is resynthesized in this part of the process.

lactic acid: Compound produced by anaerobic glycolysis that has been linked to the burning sensation you get in your legs after hard interval work and other symptoms of muscular exhaustion.

lateral pitch: Also called outboard pitch. Refers to the port-starboard pitch built into the oarlock allowing fore-and-aft pitch to decrease as the oar moves from the catch to the release.

layback: The act of leaning one's back toward the bow at the finish. Should not be more than 10 or 15 degrees past vertical.

load: The amount of leverage built into the rig you are using. Load is a function of the span, or distance between the pins, and the inboard.

LSD (long slow distance): Term describing steady-state pieces lasting over 30 minutes.

logbook: A journal used to record your daily training activity, your goals and objectives, rigging information, and any other information you feel is important. Should be saved forever.

lunge or lunging: See dive.

maximal oxygen uptake or

maxVO2: The most oxygen one can use to perform work. Can be measured in terms of milliliters of oxygen per kilogram of body weight (ml/kg) or total liters. Measurements are given in terms of oxygen consumed per minute.

motor unit: The individual motor nerve and the muscle cells it innervates.

muscular endurance: The ability of a muscle to perform repeated contractions over a long period of time, like sculling.

National Association of Amateur Oarsmen (NAA): The name of the original US amateur rowing organization. Changed to US ROWING to keep in step with modern times.

National Women's Rowing Association: The original governing body for women's rowing in the US, no longer active due to a merger with the NAAO.

neuromuscular junction: The joint of a muscle and the nerve innervating it.

oarlock: The device that holds the oar at the end of the rigger.

octuple: Eight scullers in one boat.

oxidative: Refers to the removal of electrons during a chemical process.

oxygen debt:
The amount of oxygen consumed immediately after work has ceased that is greater than that normally consumed at rest. The oxygen debt is produced as a result of the anaerobic energy systems.

outboard: The distance from the face of the button to the tip of the blade.

paddle: To scull at very light pressure.

peak: The physiological state where you are at the top of your conditioning cycle. Careful planning is needed to ensure this occurs at the appropriate time.

petite finals: The second level of finals usually held at major regattas to determine seventh through twelfth place.

piece: A term referring to any period of work performed in a shell. Might be a ten-minute piece, a 500-meter piece, or a 20-stroke piece.

pinch: What occurs when one's oars are at too acute an angle to the boat, resulting in the force exerted on the oars "pinching" the boat. Can occur at the catch or the release.

pH: A measure of acidity/alkalinity; blood pH is normally 7.4.

phosphagen system: One of the anaerobic energy systems; this system is used to produce short bursts of energy lasting only a few seconds.

pin: The metal cylinder the oarlock swivels on.

pitch: The angle of the oarlock and/or the angle built into the oar.

port: When looking toward the bow, the left side of the boat. Scullers have a backwards perspective on things, so it is actually to your right.

power: The performance of work over time. Can be expressed as a kilogram/meter/second (moving a kilogram a distance of one meter in one second).

power ten or twenty,

etc.: A series of strokes at an increased power level, usually performed without increasing the rating.

protein: A basic food containing amino acids.

pulmonary: Refers to the lungs and respiratory system.

pyruvic acid: The end-product of aerobic glycolysis, used as an input for the Krebs cycle.

quad: Abbreviation for quadruple sculls.

race plan: The plan or strategy one develops for a race that is designed to produce the desired outcome.

rating: The number of strokes per minute one rows.

recovery: Refers to that part of the stroke cycle where the blades are out of the water.

regatta: A series of several boat races.

release: The point in the stroke cycle where the oars come out of the water at the finish, or "release" the water.

repechage: Literally, second chance. The repechage, or rep, is the race after the heat for scullers who did not win their heat. The rest of the semifinals or final are filled with boats qualifying through the reps.

rigger: The metal or carbon-fiber arms projecting from the side of the boat to which the oarlocks are attached. Also refers to the person who fixes boats and sets them up for rowing and sculling.

rowing: Refers to using one oar per person as opposed to sculling's two oars per person. Also used to refer to both sports.

rush: A technical error caused by sliding too quickly and abruptly toward the stern.

scull: Technically, the oar scullers use. Also refers to the act of sculling, e.g., "Do you scull?"

settle: Refers to the part of the race (or other piece) where you decrease the rating from the initial high stroke to a lower pace that you will maintain until the final sprint.

shell: Another term for a rowing or sculling boat.

shooting the slide: A technical error evidenced by movement of the slide toward the bow without moving the oar handles at the same rate.

skeg: See fin.

sky: Technical error caused by dropping the hands at the catch, resulting in the blades heading skyward.

slide: The seat you place your rear end on when you scull. Also refers to the motion on the slide, as in "slow your slide."

slow twitch (ST): Refers to a muscle fiber that is specifically adapted to perform work aerobically.

somatotype: The body type of a human.

span: The distance between the pins. Also called spread.

specificity of training: The principal basis for constructing a training program to improve one's performance in a specific sport or activity. Refers to performing activities designed to improve one's performance in that sport specifically.

spread: See span.

stakeboat: The dinghy anchored at the starting line that holds a person who in turns holds your stern as you sit at the line waiting for the starting commands.

starboard: The right side of the boat when looking at it from the stern; the left from a sculler's perspective.

steady state: Long, aerobic work.

sternpost: The post sticking up from the tip of the stern through which the rudder shaft slides. Also can refer to the terminal end of the stern even if there is no actual post.

strength: The force that a muscle can exert against resistance in one maximal effort.

stroke: Refers to the person in a team boat who sits in the stern and sets the pace. Most definitely not a command called by a coxswain.

stroke volume: The amount of blood that can be pumped by the left ventricle of the heart in one contraction.

square blades: Positioning blades perpendicular to the water.

swing: The almost-mystical sweet spot of team and individual sculling. Swing occurs when the entire crew is moving perfectly in unison and the boat seems to be moving very fast without much effort. If you have swing, you'll know it. It does not happen very often.

target heart rate: The heart rate at which one works during a specific exercise period.

technique work: Refers to a practice, or part of a practice, that concentrates on a particular aspect or aspects of sculling technique.

through-the-pin: A rigging term referring to the horizontal distance from a line connecting the pins to the front of the seat.

toe: To steer a boat by moving one's foot. The right shoe is mounted on a pivot and cables run from the toe of the shoes to the rudder at the stern.

tracks: The metal channels in which the wheels of the slide travel.

Type I cells: See slow twitch.

Type II cells: See fast twitch.

Type IIa cells (FTO): Fast-twitch cells that, probably through training, have developed an increased ability to produce energy aerobically. Also referred to as fast-twitch oxidative-glycolytic.

vasoconstriction: A decrease in the diameter of a blood vessel leading to a decrease in blood flow to that particular area.

washbox: The part of the gunwale that comes to a V at the bow end of the tracks.

wash out: Motion of the blade whereby the blade comes out of the water prematurely. Can be caused by poor technique or rigging error.

wetted-surface area: That part of the boat that is wet when the sculler is sitting in the boat. Used to calculate friction and drag.

weight limits: Refers to FISA's lower limits on boat weights used in international competition.

wherry: A broad-beamed, shorter sculling boat that is quite stable and suitable for novice scullers.

work: Force over distance; for example, moving one kilogram one meter. Also refers to the bottom of the inside face of the oarlock, as in "the height of the work."

Index